PILO

Also by Errol Brathwaite

NOVELS
Fear in the Night
An Affair of Men
Long Way Home
The Flying Fish
The Needle's Eye
The Evil Day
The Flame Box

TRAVEL/GEOGRAPHICAL
The Companion Guide to the North Island
The Companion Guide to the South Island
The Companion Guide to Westland
The Companion Guide to Otago, Southland and Stewart Island
The Beauty of New Zealand
The Beauty of New Zealand's North Island
The Beauty of New Zealand's South Island
Historic New Zealand
New Zealand and its People
The Beauty of Waikato and Bay of Plenty
Beautiful New Zealand

HISTORIES/MISCELLANEOUS
The House Built Upon a Rock
Morning Flight
Sixty Red Nightcaps
Just Looking (with John Haycroft)

PILOT ON THE RUN

The Epic Escape from Occupied France
of Flight Sergeant
L.S.M. (Chalky) White RNZAF

As told to
ERROL BRATHWAITE

HUTCHINSON
NEW ZEALAND

Century Hutchinson New Zealand Ltd.
An Imprint of the Century Hutchinson Group
32-34 View Road, P.O. Box 40-086, Glenfield, Auckland

Century Hutchinson Ltd.
62-65 Chandos Place, Covent Garden, London WC2N 4 NW.

Century Hutchinson Australia Pty, Ltd.
16-22 Church Street, Hawthorne, Melbourne, Victoria 3122
89-91 Albion Street, Surry Hills, Sydney, N.S.W. 2010

Century Hutchinson South Africa Pty. Ltd.
P.O. Box 337, Bergvlei 2012, South Africa

First Published 1986

Produced by ken pounder ltd., Auckland
Typeset by Sabagraphics Ltd., Christchurch
Printed and bound in Hong Kong

I.S.B.N. (Cased) 0 09 165150 6
I.S.B.N. (Limp) 0 09 165151 4

A bomber type's grateful tribute to all fighter escorts — especially those who didn't make it, and those who had to take the long way home.

Special thanks are due to:
RNZAF Photographic Flights, Ohakea and Wigram, for assistance and permission to publish official photographs Nos 3, 4, 5, 6, 7 and 12.
Group Captain D.J. Scott, for advice and photographs No's 8 and 14.
Mrs Pauline Hocking, for assistance with French translation.
Mrs Hilde Otley, for assistance with German translation.

Cover design, painting, and map by James Sanders.

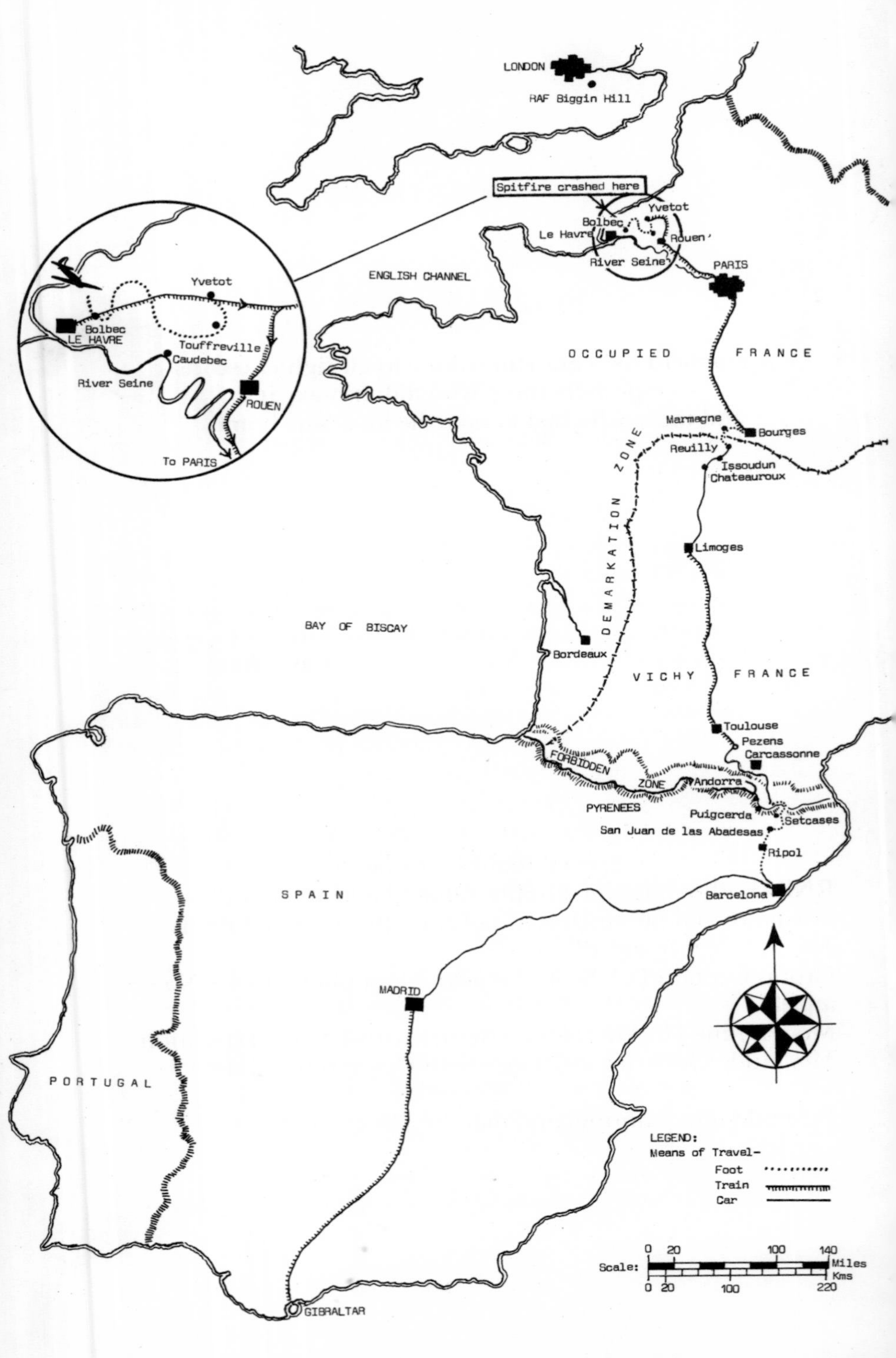

LONDON
RAF Biggin Hill
Spitfire crashed here
Yvetot
Bolbec
Le Havre
Rouen
River Seine
PARIS
ENGLISH CHANNEL
Yvetot
Bolbec
LE HAVRE
Touffreville
Caudebec
River Seine
ROUEN
To PARIS
OCCUPIED FRANCE
Marmagne
Bourges
Reuilly
Issoudun
Chateauroux
DEMARKATION ZONE
Limoges
BAY OF BISCAY
Bordeaux
VICHY FRANCE
Toulouse
Pezens
Carcassonne
FORBIDDEN ZONE
Andorra
PYRENEES
Puigcerda
Setcases
San Juan de las Abadesas
Ripol
Barcelona
SPAIN
MADRID
PORTUGAL
GIBRALTAR
LEGEND:
Means of Travel-
Foot
Train
Car
Scale:
0 20 100 140 Miles
0 20 100 220 Kms

FOREWORD

By Group Captain D.J. Scott, D.S.O., O.B.E., D.F.C. & BAR Commander of the Order of Orange Nassau, French Croix de Geurre & Palm, Belgian Croix de Geurre & Palm, M.I.D.

Typhoon and Spitfire pilots had little in common, but from a Typhoon Commander's point of view, visits to Spitfire squadrons often had their rewards. One evening I dropped into Westhampnett — an airfield near Chichester — to see 485 New Zealand Spitfire Squadron, and was invited to stay and attend a party in the Sergeants' Mess.

I had hardly entered the building when Dumbo Grant, the squadron C.O., introduced me to a powerfully built sergeant pilot whose shoulders were so wide they appeared to be bursting out of his battledress. Sergeant Leslie Samuel McQueen White — or Chalky, as he was better known — put out a hand that resembled a smoked ham and felt like the blunt end of a stable broom. Clutching my own hand in a vice-like grip, he treated my arm as if it was the village pump. While my fingers screamed out for mercy, a broad smile crossed his face, pushing his eyes into two slits and reminding me of a picture I had once seen of an Eskimo chieftain. I was thankful when he released his grip and reached out across a well stocked table for a bottle of beer. No fancy tools were necessary. He casually pulled the cap off the bottle with his teeth, took a long swig, and after a hearty belch, handed me what was left of its contents. "Cheers", he said in a gravelly voice.

He didn't wait for my thanks. Two sergeant pilots began a heated argument on the other side of the table, and Chalky, without further ado, detached himself from Dumbo and me and moved off in their direction. I couldn't hear what was being said above the noise of the party, but the two misfits, on being spoken to by Chalky, quickly disappeared — and in different directions. With my hand still smarting, I had good reason to feel impressed; nor was there any necessity for Dumbo to remind me who was the boss in the Sergeants' Mess at Westhampnett. Chalky looked more like a lumberjack than a Spitfire pilot, although I was not surprised when Dumbo said he came from a sheep farm in the Waikaka Valley in Southland. I could immediately picture his tousled head and long arms in the shearing shed, or the sweat, pain and blasphemy of a high country muster.

Two years were to pass before I saw him again. It was at Merville Airfield near Lille in the Pas de Calais where I had my four squadrons of rocket firing Typhoons. He was by this time a flight lieutenant and wearing a well merited D.F.C. I had heard of his exploits of course, as Chalky was no ordinary run-of-the-mill fighter pilot. I knew he had been shot down in the late summer of 1943 while helping to cover a bombing raid on the German airfield at Beaumont-le-Roger. As he said, "a lot had happened since our last meeting". Three of his Squadron mates were also shot down on the same mission; Jack Rae, Gentleman Jack, who had done so well over Malta in the previous year, Pilot Officer F.D. Clark from Wanganui, and a Dunedin boy, Flight Lieutenant M.G. Sutherland.

At the time, I had a feeling that Chalky was indestructible, and if any of the four made their escape to England it would be him. To be shot down in broad daylight above the outskirts of Le Havre was a big enough handicap in itself. To escape through the Atlantic Wall, through occupied France and over the Pyrénées and into Spain was the equivalent of climbing the world's highest mountain without oxygen. But no Everest was too high for Chalky, for it was he who made the grade. By the time he reached England he had completed a journey of nearly two thousand miles — every yard of which had been fraught with danger.

PILOT ON THE RUN is a remarkable story about a remarkable man. A man whose courage and devotion to duty has set an example that will live forever in the annals of the Royal Air Force.

Desmond J. Scott.

1.

It was a glorious day.

At home, on such a beautiful Sunday, people used to load up the car with picnic baskets and head for the nearest river — Dusky Forest, maybe, where the kids could splash and shout and make the sun-spangled river laugh, while Mum spread out on the rug an enormous feast of salad and bacon-and-egg pie, and scones, and meat sandwiches, and sliced ham; and Dad gathered sticks, and built a fireplace of river stones, and lit a fire to boil the billy to make strong, smoky tea.

Or, maybe, if it was around Christmas, the days, Sunday included, were sweated out in the shed, bent double over a succession of stiff-necked, squirming old ewes, with the hand sweeping unerringly around her shifting contours as the indignant old lady tried to wriggle, guiding the clippers, making her heavy fleece flop open like an unbuttoned coat, onto the grease-slick floor.

But not today.

For one thing, this brilliant afternoon was in August, and August here was early autumn. At home, just now, it was entirely possible that pockets of snow still patched the hillsides, and almost certain that newborn lambs were arriving with sleet and hailstorms, and shivering in the last blasts of departing winter. For another thing, this was no picnic. This was war.

Even so, war is not all unrelieved fury. For Flight Sergeant Chalky White, heading out on bomber escort duty, it was possible to be moderately comfortable, to have a feeling of wellbeing, as when sitting in the admittedly not over-roomy cockpit of a Mark IX Spitfire, feeling the sun coming warm through the bubble canopy, and hearing the Merlin singing sweet and even. You could look below, and see the patchwork quilt, the endearing fields and valleys and woods in the soft haze of England, imperturbable, as though the war was a bad dream, and the real, unchanging, enduring things were here, beneath this brilliant sky, and in those immemorial woods and ageless fields. At times like this it was easy to fall in with the mood of Gillespie McGee, the young pilot-poet, who wrote ecstatically of "slipping the surly bonds of earth," and "topping the windswept clouds with easy grace." But it is extremely unlikely that Chalky White, late of the Waikaka Valley, South Otago, was even vaguely familiar with the poem.

You understand, Flight Sergeant Leslie Samuel McQueen White had never had much time for poetry. That is not to say that he despised it. It was simply that there had never been time or money for frills in his education.

When his schooling began, it was a case of riding his pony three and a half miles to the nearest school — after he'd finished the chore of milking three cows by hand. It doesn't sound much, when you say it quickly, but this is a five-year-old child we're talking about — a very small boy, riding gamely in all weathers. Riding in a gale, he was actually blown from his horse, and his left arm and collar bone were broken. (He received no medical attention for it. In those days you only called in the doctor — you could only afford to call him in — for something serious. Sixty-odd years afterwards, the arm still gives him a bit of trouble, Chalky admits. The collar bone fracture he never suspected until an X-ray revealed it quite recently.)

He had good teachers and bad teachers, teachers from whom he could learn, and teachers from whom he could not. He doesn't, nowadays, seek to lay blame, or to spend endless hours writing to the newspapers to protest against his lack of scholastic achievement, and his wasted potential. He doesn't believe that he's wasted anything. He would never use the word himself, but Chalky White has always been a pragmatist — which is to say that, in his philosophy, the useful results of the application of an idea are the test of that idea's truth. For example, he suffered under what he called a "bad" teacher. His idea was that for the beatings he endured and the petty tyrannies and frequent humiliations he had suffered, he should give that teacher a hiding — with an elder brother's help. They did. The result was that thereafter, the young White had to ride another three miles daily, to the next nearest school, where at least he was able to catch up sufficiently to earn his Competency, and, armed with this, he went to secondary school. Here, however, he discovered that Competency was not only regarded less favourably than Proficiency, but also meant that from here on, his education would no longer be free. When his elder brothers and sister went through the system, it didn't matter too much. They were simply, like many farmer's sons and daughters, sent to college. But by the time Chalky's turn came around, the country was in the grip of the Great Depression, and there was no money to spare for a boarding school or a private education. He, therefore, had to go to the nearest District High School, which was at Gore; which now meant that he began his day — after morning chores were done — with an eleven-mile horseback ride. He endured this for four years, until he was expelled, for one reason and another.

At the age of fifteen, Chalky joined the workforce. On a sheep and cattle station, he learned to shear sheep, and very soon sheared his first hundred. With that goal behind him, he worked for the next few years as a shearer in New Zealand and Australia; and between seasons he worked in freezing works in both countries.

Perhaps, after all, this was the education that Chalky White was going to need, not just to make his living, but for very survival.

He was in Australia when war broke out in 1939, and he promptly volunteered for the RAAF.

In any air force, as every airman knows, things must be done correctly, in order to avoid ultimate confusion. It doesn't, entirely, but at least it's an orderly confusion. You learn that, from your very first contact. Always do things correctly, through channels. In practical terms it means, amongst other things, that you cannot, even in wartime, go breasting up to the recruitment counter and say, "Here I am. Where do you want me to start?" There are Regulations, all sorts of them, which have to be observed. So Chalky White, who hates hanging about, found that he had to wait until his application had been processed.

Napoleon, with whom it is probable that Chalky White would have got along famously, and by whom he would most likely have been rapidly promoted, based his tactics on the aphorism, "Attack at all points, and then see."

Chalky, although he never put it into quite such a neat package of words, believed that in any given situation, you should pitch straight in and sort out the details later. In this instance, there could be no question of hanging about in Australia, waiting to be processed. So he returned to New Zealand, and applied to join the RNZAF.

He might not have been so hopeful of speedy results had he known that New Zealand's Air Force had just undertaken to provide, each year, for the duration of the war, 2882 aircrew. For an air force that had been, just weeks previously, a tiny force numbered in mere hundreds, all trades, that was a colossal task, and it took a little time to get into gear. Chalky had to wait even longer than he would have had he stuck with his original idea of joining the RAAF.

So, all things considered, he was an extremely unlikely candidate for the position of Spitfire pilot — except that his life experience to date had endowed him with one priceless advantage. Chalky White believed in himself. And he believed that a man can do anything he sets his mind to — one way or another.

Enlisted at last, he was sent to Canada, to train under the Empire Air Training Scheme. There he received his advanced flying training on a pugnacious-looking, bulbous-nosed little cabin monoplane, the Cessna Crane. And then, having gained his wings, he was sent with a batch of other brand new pilots to England.

The Spitfire, of course, was the glamour aircraft of the war, the machine which gripped the imagination, and beckoned aircrew trainees through seemingly endless hours of tedious classroom training in such palpitatingly unexciting subjects as navigation, meteorology, engines and basic airmanship. A Spitfire was what Chalky White wanted to fly — yet here he was, with his logbook entries indicating that he had been trained, and built up his flying hours on, multi-engined aircraft; and that, of course, should have destined him for a bomber squadron.

But when this draft of newly-trained pilots was separated into two lines, one of multi-engine pilots and one of single-engine pilots, Chalky felt that he was being given a final choice. So he fell in with the single-engine boys; and, presumably because no RAF processing clerk would have believed that anyone would have the temerity to join the Wrong Queue, it was apparently assumed that the single-engine line was the one into which he had been directed by Someone Higher Up.

So, here he was, on this beautiful afternoon, Green 3, sub-section leader of four Spitfires of 485 Squadron on bomber escort duty, with the German airfield at Beaumont-le-Roger as their target. The White Cliffs passed beneath him, and there was the Channel, glinting in the late afternoon sunshine, looking for all the world like a vast sheet of crumpled, green-blue, white-flecked tinfoil, not so very far below.

Bombing German fighter airfields was not unlike poking a stick into a hornets' nest and giving it a good stir. But you try not to anticipate, on these occasions. You try to keep your mind on the job, working through the job minute by minute. You do deliberately a multitude of small tasks, like checking your fuel consumption, manifold pressure, oil, coolant. Over the Channel, heading for France, you keep a wide-eyed watch on the surrounding air. "Beware of the Hun in the Sun," a thousand reminder posters in every crew room, ready room, hangar, repair bay, kept telling you, and you heeded it now, very seriously. And, as sub-section leader, you kept a check on your sub-section, on the rest of the section and, as an escort, a shepherd's eye on the bomber formation. You kept physically and mentally busy.

Maybe, though, as you crossed the French coast, your mouth became a touch dry, and there was possibly a tiny beading of sweat on your upper lip. If so, you told yourself emphatically that it was just another job, that maybe Jerry wouldn't react too violently this time, and that, come what may, it would be over pretty smartly, and you'd be back home about an hour and a half after take-off. Maybe those kind of thoughts were in Chalky White's mind. Or maybe not. All he remembers is that just then all hell broke loose.

The formation was jumped by eighty-plus Huns, and in seconds the air was full of aircraft, diving, zooming, whirling in a mad aerial saraband. The radio exploded into a gabble of shouted warnings, punctuated with hoarse bleeping as two or more transmitters came on together and jammed each other.

Chalky found himself on the tail of an FW190. He followed it around in a long curve, opening up the tap, cramming on the revs until the 1600hp Merlin screamed, and the wind howled and thrummed over the cockpit canopy. He tucked in behind the FW's tail and gave it a long squirt. Two 20mm cannon and four .303 Browning machineguns punched, thrashed, tore at the FW. Pieces flew from it. White vapour streamed from it, and then smoke; and orange fire blossomed and licked along the fuselage. A landing wheel dropped down from its recess in the wing, the FW flopped over onto its back, nosed down and spun earthwards.

Chalky looked around for his wing man, couldn't see him, looked back, stuffed the nose down to avoid collision with an aircraft which rocketed away overhead. He heard the chump-chump of shells hitting his fuselage, aft, and took violent evasive action. A glance over his shoulder showed him a Focke-Wulf boring in. At least three others were jockeying for position. Wing leading edges winked, and 20mm shells punched hard against the armour plate at his back. Glass shattered in the instrument panel, and he felt the nettle-burn sting of tiny slivers of shell. Jagged-edged holes appeared in the mullet-head cowling. The engine temperature began immediately to climb. His cooling system had been hit.

The radio was dead, also. No question of calling for help. He hauled the Spit around in a turn which pressed him down into his seat, and pulled at his face, and weighted his hands with invisible lead. Then he nosed down and streaked towards the coast, pushing his badly hit aircraft hard.

He won clear of the mêlée, and gave himself time to think.

Even as he crossed the coast, the temperature gauge needle went off the clock. In a minute or two at most, the engine would seize — and there was still the Channel to cross.

There was only one things for it. Turn around and head inland.

Then eight more Huns appeared, and Chalky, with his engine overheated and no one near at hand to help, took them on. As he figured it, he had no choice. Four of them turned off after another crippled Spitfire, but four of them came at Chalky — and he got one.

But then his engine seized with a judder that threatened to tear it from its bearers, and he headed for the ground, smartly. Three or four miles inland on the outskirts of Le Havre, a city about the size of Christchurch, he sorted out what seemed to be a reasonably flat field, and brought the crippled Spitfire down.

Saying it like that makes it sound easy enough. But this was to be a wheels-up landing on an unknown surface, without the benefit of an engine. There would be no question of overshoot-and-go-around-again if closer inspection revealed that the ground was not suitable after all. Also, a high-performance fighter like the Spitfire is an entirely different proposition to a modern light aircraft. For one thing, the cockpit was small, and full of knobbly and sharp things, notably the reflector sight just in front of the pilot's face. For another, such an aircraft stormed through the air like an arrow from a bow, rather than floating around like a powered thistle-down. If you want to set it down fairly precisely, dead-stick, you need hair-trigger reactions and nice judgement. You don't want to land too fast, or you could end up in a total wreck, very dead. You don't want to lose forward speed too quickly, or you could plunge in from a great height. You feel your way in, putting on a bit of flap — not enough to act as a brake in mid-air, but enough to give you that extra bit of wing area, that extra bit of lift, to compensate as much as maybe for your loss of forward speed.

Of course, the landing's going to be rough, no matter how good you are. You aim at the kind of landing which would, if you had your wheels down, be a perfect three-pointer. The ideal is to have your tail wheel hit first, to brake you a bit, so that when your belly hits the turf, if the nose hits a minor obstruction or two it won't dig in and flip you over onto your back.

And you have to do all this even though you are still tense from combat and, in Chalky's case, have two eager Huns following you down, still pumping shells into your aircraft.

Chalky did it. It did dig its nose in, and because it was coming in at about 190mph, it stood on its nose for a moment, a heart-stopping half-minute, before flopping back onto its belly on the torn turf. Some considerable time later, a friend of Chalky's in a German POW camp, leafing through a German aviation magazine, came across a picture of Chalky's aircraft, unmistakeably coded F-OU. The photograph, captioned *"Abgeschusene englische Spitfire."* ("Shot-down English Spitfire"), is evidence of how successfully Chalky put it down in that French paddock.

Not that he had much time for self-congratulation. As the very existence of the photograph shows, he didn't have time to destroy his machine. The two Focke-Wulfs were circling close overhead, probably to see if he had survived, and to get confirmation of the "kill." And two German soldiers who had materialised in the middle distance were running towards the aircraft.

Chalky attempted to slide the canopy open. It seemed to be stuck, perhaps because the fuselage had twisted or distorted, or maybe because the runners were damaged by shell splinters. He grabbed it in his two huge, leg-of-mutton fists and wrenched it back by main strength. Then he scrambled out, leaving Mae West life-jacket, parachute and revolver behind, and made his way at the double over the brow of a nearby hill.

Some French peasants happened to be out walking in the vicinity. (Great walkers, these French, Chalky comments.) They were probably out for their Sunday afternoon constitutional, obviously an imperturbable lot. Nothing, not the Germans, not the war, not life-and-death battles between fighters overhead, not even a downed and desperate British airman looming breathlessly over their horizon in full battledress and flying boots, was going to come between them and their Sunday afternoon stroll. They made no fuss, showed no undue excitement. They simply, silently, pointed to some bushes where *l'aviateur anglais* might conceal himself from *les sales Boche*. And on they walked, as if nothing untoward had happened.

Chalky found this reaction on their part oddly cheering. They were prepared to help. And, what's more, they managed to do so by sign language — which was just as well, because he certainly didn't have any French. It wasn't part of a shearer's essential equipment, in outback Australia or Southland.

So Chalky hid in the bushes; and as he lay there, the bombers droned overhead on their way home, thirty-six Marauders, all present and correct. That part of his job had been taken care of adequately. Now all he had to do was to get home himself.

Chalky White is not a man to endure inactivity for very long. When he figured that the neighbourhood had settled down, he emerged. He knew exactly what he had to do, now. The encounter with the helpful peasants had encouraged him. Obviously, they still looked upon themselves as allies. All he had to do, was to make for the first Frenchman he saw, and explain his predicament.

As far as it went, he was right. But when you have no French, getting your story across, and receiving helpful hints, is a protracted business necessitating much animated sign language, and it is apt to make you conspicuous at a distance from which your uniform would be no sort of giveaway at all. That, and the fact that all Frenchmen wore berets, and Chalky was bare-headed.

The next Frenchmen he spotted were on the outskirts of the small village of Bolbec, in the midst of the massively fortified swath of country known as the Atlantic Wall. Bolbec was occupied by Germans, two of whom spotted him from the window of a nearby house. They came tumbling forth, fully armed and accoutred, followed by a small and curious horde of their comrades. They menaced Chalky with rifle and bayonet, shouted at him, prodded him with a rifle butt, and marched him to a nearby farmhouse.

Chalky White, on that fine August afternoon, became a prisoner of the Third Reich.

2.

The initial interrogation was not too rigorous. The officer tended to shout a bit, but from what Chalky had seen in the past twenty minutes, that was apparently a Hun habit. When a German wanted you to know that he had a little authority, he barked. The lesser the authority, the louder the bark. Sheepdogs did it, Chalky thought sourly, so why not Germans? The ones who had brought him to this farmhouse were in the huntaway class, and even the officer was not exactly one of your strong-eyes. But Chalky answered every question blandly with the reiterated statement that his number was NZ413919, his name was White, Leslie Samuel McQueen, and his rank was Flight Sergeant.

Somewhere in the surrounding countryside at this time were three more Spitfires and four German FW190s; three more British pilots presumably roaming about, and four German pilots possibly in need of succour of some kind. Probably the harrassed officer felt that this kind of thing shouldn't happen to a man who had at last won himself a soft Army of Occupation billet in a peaceful rural environment. Frustrated, he made some dark remark, the precise meaning of which was lost on Chalky, but the tone of which, in any army in the world, plainly signified: "Take him away, Sar'-Major. I'll deal with him later." Chalky had heard it often enough in his own brief and turbulent military career to recognise it.

So the captive airman was consigned to the care of a single-armed guard, and the officer and every other German in the place went pounding off to take part in the search and rescue operations, their Sunday afternoon irredeemably ruined by these inconvenient airmen.

Chalky sat uncomfortably in a chair and looked amiably at the guard, against whom he had nothing personal. The guard gazed stolidly back. All in all, Chalky thought, it was a scenario which was bound very soon to get boring. The Germans were boring. The farmhouse was boring. The blowfly buzzing tiredly around the light was boring. Prisoner-of-war camp would almost certainly be even more boring.

They had searched Chalky perfunctorily, an all-over patting to make sure he possessed no lethal weapons, perhaps not understanding that the term is relative. At all events, they missed his little set of escape maps printed on silk, and the two compasses that he carried in an oiled linen bag with the maps in the inside pocket of his battledress jacket; and they had briefly examined and returned — possibly with a tailor-made smoker's contempt for roll-your-owns — his tin of tobacco, his papers and his matches.

These Chalky now brought forth. He proceeded to roll himself a cigarette, a process which seemed to fascinate the guard; and he lit it and inhaled luxuriously. After what he had just been through, he figured, he had earned a smoke, and he now set about having it with every evidence of enjoyment.

You can say what you like about roll-your owns, Chalky would say, but the fact remains that the tobacco, not being gucked up with saltpetre or toasted to the point of aridity, is far more fragrant, far sweeter in a smoker's nostrils, than any tailormade.

Whatever the truth of that, the guard's eyes betrayed a tobacco hunger, and he looked longingly at the tobacco tin, and then at Chalky, and essayed a smile. He didn't actually go so far as to put down his rifle when Chalky proffered the tobacco tin, but he did sling it from his shoulder as he stepped forward to accept his prisoner's invitation. Chalky concedes that it wasn't deliberate dereliction of duty, but merely the reflex action of a smoker who has had to make do on French cigarettes or on some ersatz product. Such a smoker wouldn't have found it difficult to persuade himself that enmity doesn't have to be personal.

For Chalky, however, enmity had nothing to do with it. War, to him, was war. He was bored with inactivity; and beneath his boredom, he was very, very angry — at the Germans for his predicament, but even more at himself for having been caught so soon. He stood up smiling, the tobacco tin held out in one hand; and as he stood, he brought up his left hand in a haymaker that started near his ankles. The guard subsided bloodily against the wall.

Chalky picked up and pocketed his makings and stepped outside into the warmth of the lovely evening.

There was no one in sight, but there were Germans just outside the farmyard, on the road. The sound of their marching feet told him that they were returning to the house. He ran out into the farmyard, searching frantically for a way out. There was a high wall on one side, and a tall barn on the other, and across the end was a dense macrocarpa hedge.

The marching feet and chivvying bark of an NCO were coming closer. Chalky looked at the barn, rejected it as too obvious a hiding place. The wall was too high for him to scale, the hedge too dense for easy penetration.

He ran to a corner of the house and peered around. There was a gateway which opened onto the road. He darted back to the other corner and found that on that side of the yard, the barn was joined to the house by an outbuilding, possibly a dairy or a laundry or a storeroom of some kind. That also would be too obvious a hiding place. But against the wall of the house stood a wooden rain barrel.

Inside the house, the guard stirred and groaned. Around the corner, from the road gate, jackboots were clumping into the yard. With seconds to spare, Chalky lifted the lid of the barrel, climbed in and squatted down, replacing the lid over his head.

There was just enough water in the barrel to wet the seat of his trousers, and the crouching posture he had to adopt to fit his six foot frame into that impossibly confined space was fiendishly uncomfortable. He heard the Germans halt before the back door, and he waited for the inevitable outcry when the guard was discovered. It began in about fifteen seconds, but to Chalky, scrunched up in the barrel, it seemed longer. He remained there, determinedly motionless, his discomfort quickly though not completely overshadowed by the adrenalin-exciting experience of watching through a crack between the barrel staves as thoroughly aroused Germans poked about the barn and the macrocarpa hedge and, his ears told him, the house and outbuildings. He saw them jab bayonets into the hedge, and even into that indispensible adjunct to a French farmyard, the manure heap, and he fully expected a bayonet to come probing through the barrel staves, right into his ribs. But, incredibly, none of them seemed to think of that. The barrel, obviously, was one of those pieces of furniture to which people had becomed so accustomed that it was, to all intents and purposes, invisible.

After a noisy hour, when the shadows had begun to spread from the corners of the farmyard and deepen the descending dusk, they desisted at last. An NCO paraded them in the yard, around the corner, and marched them with Teutonic precision to their various billets and, presumably, their evening meal.

Chalky waited for a further hour. He would have preferred to wait even longer, for the lesson of his capture was not lost on him. Impatience was fatal in the serious business of evading capture. It was his hastiness in leaving his hiding place that had got him into this spot in the first place. He must not act so precipitately again, but must bide his time, work out each move thoroughly before he made it.

He judged he had reached a point-of-no-return situation. If he emerged now, he might well bump into a Hun. Ideally, he should give them time to go to bed and fall asleep. But if he squatted here, with his backside in this cold water for much longer, he might not be able to get out unaided at all. He was already suffering from painful cramps. He had to move now, before he lost the power of motion. He lifted the lid carefully, and quietly but stiffly eased himself out of his hiding place.

He had decided that there could be no question of leaving via the farmyard gateway. If, as he suspected, this was some kind of unit headquarters, there was bound to be a sentry.

So, instead, he went to the macrocarpa hedge, which proved to be every bit as fine a specimen as he had first thought it to be. Clever, these French, he told himself. And thrifty. Wire fences cost money. A good, thick macrocarpa hedge allowed passage to farmyard cats and free-ranging chooks, but denied passage to cows and sheep, and baffled even the catholic palate of a goat. Chalky eased into it, pushed harder, tore and wriggled and struggled, making what seemed to his fearful ears enough noise to waken the dead. When he was through it, scratched and sticky in patches with its gum, and stood in the open field, he took a deep breath and began to run. He ran as fast as his legs would carry him, encased as they were in clumsy flying boots. He stumbled and panted across the Normandy countryside, driven by a prickling of urgency that was barely controlled fear, and could easily have turned into blind panic; for he had no illusions regarding his probable fate should these particular Germans catch him again, after what he had done to their comrade. At the very least, he would be in for an exceedingly rough time. More likely, they would shoot him on sight.

He stopped running at last and stood still, looking about him, regaining his breath. Running blindly, he reminded himself, was foolish. If he was going to get home, he was going to have to formulate a plan, plot some sort of course. Chalky White, on that dark August night, had given the Third Reich the proverbial mitten, and he had no intention of falling into its hands, ever again. Not just because of what he had done to the guard, either. The fact was, Chalky had Jewish blood in him, and they were apt to be very rough on Jews, as everyone knew. But the real driving force, the head of steam that empowered him, after all he had been through, to give it his best effort, was his anger, smouldering at no great depth below the surface.

He could scarcely see his hand in front of his face. The moon had not yet risen, and it was very dark. Town-dwellers in particular seldom have much conception of real darkness. In town, at night, there is always a great deal of light. Even in the country, in Chalky's lifelong experience, there were generally pinpoints from distant farmhouses, or at least the skyglow over surrounding towns or cities. But this was Europe, and this was wartime. Even the city of Le Havre did not betray its presence in the slightest degree.

He tried to tell himself that that was good, because in such deep darkness he could move openly without fear of being seen. But he knew that darkness would inevitably slow him up and this added to his anger. Of course, the moon would rise in an hour or two, he told himself. And that was good because it would help him to move faster without appreciably adding to the risk of his being spotted. The only question was, in which direction should he move? It would be all too easy to run blindly in a circle and fetch up at his starting point.

South, he decided. Without any light, he could not read his escape maps, and he strove to remember the maps in the ready room back at Biggin Hill, and the general layout of France. But he couldn't, and so he decided that it would be safe enough just to move south, which would take him deeper into France. He thought he had better make for Paris. In a city of two and a half million people, all of whom must resent the German presence like mad, it shouldn't be too difficult to find someone ready and willing to aid an escaping British airman. In any case, in such a large city, he would be one individual amongst teeming millions, and consequently much less noticeable than in a smaller centre. Even in uniform — well, there must be a multitude of uniforms moving about the streets of Paris. Maybe one more, perhaps subtly altered, would arouse no curiosity.

Paris, then. In Paris, Chalky would be able to get himself organised. And, being so inconspicuous, he might even profitably risk catching a train to the South of France, Vichy France, where, presumably, there would be no German occupation forces. And from there, he could surely slip into Spain, to the British Embassy in Madrid, maybe. Anyway, it was worth a go. Others had managed it — or so he had heard.

Right, then. He would go south. And when he was a reasonable distance from here, he would try to get help from some French peasant; a beret, maybe, and yes, most certainly — a pair of boots. His flying boots were not designed for hiking. They were supremely comfortable for lounging around the Station in winter, because they were made of soft, pliable leather, fleece-lined from toe to top. And for that reason they were ideal for flying in. They kept the feet nice and warm when dicing in the upper air, which is what they were designed to do. But that same fleecy interior precluded anything like a close or supportive fit. They tended to slop around on the feet like gumboots; and Chalky suffered from ingrowing toenails, which were already beginning to hurt.

Anyway, he thought, (having by now regained his breath), southwards he would go. The only thing was, which way was south? He had his escape kit, which included those two compasses, and he now fumbled in his innermost pockets for that small, flat linen bag. The compasses had luminous dials, and he studied one and found south, then, just to make sure, he looked at the other, which proclaimed that south was in an entirely different direction.

Possibly they were standard army prismatic compasses, which are easy enough to operate if you've been shown how. Chalky hadn't. Or maybe one of them really was faulty. Chalky decided that such was the case.

"That," he said to himself exasperatedly, "is just what I need — a duff compass to start with."

And then it occurred to him that he had no way of knowing which one was faulty. How could he check them? Against the stars? At home it would have been easy. There was always the Southern Cross, at least during the summer and autumn months. But these were northern hemisphere skies, and even the familiar constelations of Orion and the Scorpion lay along unfamiliar axes as the northern night and season progressed; and astro-navigation had never been, for Chalky, the most absorbing of subjects, anyway.

So, really, there was only one thing for a man of Chalky's temperament to do. He plucked a couple of grass stems, allotted one to each compass, drew, and kept the one to which he had allotted the drawn straw. The other he chucked away. Then, taking a reading he began to move across the fields again.

It was in that moment that he heard, shatteringly close at hand, the petulent bellow of a bull.

Only gag writers, cartoonists and Hollywood producers find bulls funny. Chalky had a farmer's healthy respect for them. The fear that he had felt as he had run from the farmhouse was as nothing to the terror he felt now as he heard the unmistakeable sound of a hoof pawing the earth, and the snorting of flaring nostrils. He stood for one frozen moment. Then he began to run, to stumble, to trip and fall and pick himself up again and pound on until his legs were leaden and his lungs bursting. He ran blindly, searching for a fence to put between himself and that bull. And he couldn't find one. It was like one of those nightmares in which one tries to run away from something, but can't make any progress. He pounded on, his flip-flopping flying boots giving his ingrown toenails seven kinds of hell, adding a limp to his already fumbling and erratic gait. But the field was endless.

His anger now began to boil over. It was too bloody much — first getting shot down by a gaggle of bloody Huns, then getting captured and having to belt a bloody sentry, and then that interminable time in the bloody rainbarrel, waiting for a bloody bayonet in the bloody ribs, and now a great, overfed bastard of a French bull — all within a short four and a half hours. Enough was e-bloody-nough.

"I'll bloody have ya!" he roared into the darkness. He knew that to stop and turn and yell a threat was pure bravado. Only the bull could possibly win that game.

Somewhere in the blackness, the bull bellowed again, as if in answer. It was some distance off, obviously not following him. In days to come, Chalky would learn that his search for a fence had been in vain because French fields were seldom fenced; and unnecessary, because French bulls were invariably tethered.

There was a glow in the sky, and he wondered what it could be. It dawned upon him all at once that it was moonglow, and that the moon was about to heave itself up over the horizon, an autumn moon, a harvest moon, as orange as a French Mimolette cheese, huge on the rim of the world, silhouetting trees and houses and low, rolling hills. There was something friendly and encouraging about the moon. Apart from the light it would give him, it was a familiar thing from his childhood, the same moon that they would see at home.

He noticed, also, that it was almost directly ahead of him, which meant, compass indication notwithstanding, that he was heading almost due east. He had thrown away the wrong compass!

Still, the night was now lighter. He could see trees and, when presently the moon stood on its edge on the horizon, he could make out the odd building.

He walked reasonably briskly, ignoring his throbbing toenails, for about eight hours. For most of that time, with the help of the bright moonlight, he made very fair progress across the fields, having decided to avoid roads as much as possible. He crossed the occasional country road and narrow lane, but for most of the distance covered, he walked on springy grass or across stubble fields and, from time to time, strips of ploughed land. He estimated his average speed at two miles an hour, and when at last he decided to stop, he reckoned that he had covered a distance of nineteen or twenty miles since his escape. But now his feet were hurting almost beyond bearing, and he was tired and hungry, and the elation he had felt when the moon rose had faded. So tired was he that even his anger had degenerated into an unreasonable grumpiness, at the sinking moon, at the uneven ground, and especially at fate for having dropped him into this mess.

For he *was* in a mess. Here he was, in a foreign country, and one, moreover crawling with Huns. He could neither speak nor read French. He had little French money — just the bit they issued before you took off on flights over France, and took from you again when you got back — and he didn't understand it or know its value. He didn't even know in what approximate direction Paris lay. He didn't begin to have the foggiest notion of how to find his way from place to place, or what his chosen destination would be like when he got there. He didn't know how to ask for shelter, food, or even help of any kind. He told himself tiredly that he would cross those bridges when they arrived.

He looked at his watch, which put the time at close to four o'clock. The moon was well down, now, and the pre-dawn darkness was deepening. Chalky looked about him.

Nearby was the dark bulk of what appeared to be a haystack. It seemed a likely place to stop, and a propitious end to the first leg of his journey. He walked over to it and discovered that it was not, after all, a haystack of the kind that he was familiar with, but simply a great pile of unthreshed wheat sheaves, which he found reasonably easy to climb. On top of it he made himself a hollow, pulled a couple of the sheaves over himself, and lay there. He was sweating, but now, having stopped driving himself, he felt the chill of the autumn night penetrating his clothing. Nevertheless, he fell instantly and deeply asleep.

3.

Chalky awoke to full daylight at about seven o'clock. From his hiding place he could see, close by, a smallish wood, which marched over the rounded top and advanced down the flank of a low hill. In his field were several piles of wheatsheaves, around them numbers of as yet unstacked stooks. And there were houses; not a village, exactly, but a small cluster of farmsteads whose fields radiated out from them. Closest, perhaps fifty yards away, was what he took to be the house to which this field belonged. It formed one side of a walled enclosure that incorporated a barn and some outbuildings, in all respects similar to the one from which he had escaped.

He was hungry. More than that, he was ravenous. His stomach grumbled at its emptiness. His first impulse, therefore, was to go and ask — in whatever way he could devise on the spur of the moment — for food. But he had learned the lesson of caution well, and decided to stay where he was until he could be reasonably sure that the house was not occupied by Germans, and that he stood a good chance of getting to it unobserved. There was doubtless a road close to the farm, perhaps just on the other side of it; and for all he knew, that wood could conceal, just within its fringe, a country lane, along which German troops might happen at an embarrassing moment.

Just the same, he was hungry. He pulled a few handfuls of grain and chewed on it, husks and all. It was not satisfying. Maybe he should go over to that house right away. Maybe the risk was justified by the need to keep up his strength.

The argument was insidious, but false. Even as Chalky was on the point of sitting up and descending from his hideaway, German trucks came speeding up the road in a cloud of dust, and stopped close to the farm. For the next nine hours, as he lay hidden, Chalky was an interested and, from time to time, apprehensive spectator as they searched for him. It was a repetition of the barrel episode, and he found it faintly amusing for as long as they kept their distance. He watched, alternating between alarm and contemptuous amusement as they unenthusiastically plodded and prodded amongst the spinneys and hedges, and went through the mechanical drills of surrounding and searching the houses. It was nerve-racking whenever they moved close to his stack; but as in the instance of the water barrel, they evidently felt that the stack was too obvious a place for a fugitive to hide in.

Most of Chalky's contempt was reserved for the officers and NCOs directing the search. It was pretty slack, he thought. In their place, he would have pulled the stacks and stooks apart, straw by straw. But then he tried to put himself in their boots. Their Sunday had been rudely interrupted, they had probably spent hours plodding over the countryside, looking for downed airmen. And even when they'd got one, he reminded himself with a flash of malicious glee, they'd gone and lost him again. Moreover one of them had probably spent most of this morning on sick parade. Chalky admitted to himself that he didn't know, that Germans might be different from the rest of humanity; but he had, nevertheless, a distinct feeling that to the Occupation Forces it must have come as a rude awakening to discover that, far from landing a soft billet with lots of beer, frauleins and spare time, they could still be called upon to work, and that the enemy could still do them an injury.

At long last, at about four o'clock in the afternoon, the chivvying and barking of NCOs ceased, and the troops formed up on the road beyond the farmhouse, and entrucked for their distant billets. That, Chalky thought, suggested that none was billeted locally. Just the same, he waited till about half past five, which seemed a likely time for them to be having their evening meal. Then he cautiously emerged from his hiding place and approached the house.

Knocking at the door was an act which in itself required the summoning up of an extra dash of courage. Courage is apt to waver when the stomach has been neglected for some thirty stressful hours. The doubts come crowding, and optimism is at a low ebb. There could, after all, be Germans. Chalky's observations suggested not, but he didn't know positively, and it is difficult, at such times, to trust one's own judgement. But Chalky the pragmatist shrugged his shoulders, raised his fist and hammered upon the door. ("Attack at all points, and then see.") Having done it, he reminded himself that he was hungry, alone, and needed help. If he didn't get help, he was probably lost anyway. He might not have done the right thing. He had done the only thing.

A woman answered his knocking. He stood there for a moment, looking at her, not knowing what to say, or how to say it if he had known. He essayed a hopeful grin, which was not answered. The woman's face was set in a taut, worried expression. He thought, from a slight change of expression around her eyes, that she was trying to smile, but could not. After all, he thought, this woman has been subjected to a house-search by Germans, just a few hours ago.

He pointed to his pilot's wings and the New Zealand flashes on his shoulders. Still she said nothing; but a man's voice behind her spoke, two brief, unintelligible syllables, and she glanced back over her shoulder and replied with almost equal brevity. Then she looked at Chalky, glanced back at the room, leaned forward and looked across the field towards the stack and the woods, then beckoned him in.

Chalky stepped warily inside. He was wound up like a steel spring, ready for anything. He stood just within the doorway, so that she had difficulty in reaching past him to shut the door, and he peered into the dark interior, his eyes slowly adjusting after the comparative brightness of the early evening outside. A man stood back against the wall by a large hutch dresser, looking at him. He was not surly, Chalky observed, but merely expressionless.

"Que voulez-vous?" the woman asked.

Chalky did not understand the words, but the intonation made it plain that she was asking him what he wanted. He pointed to his mouth, patted his stomach and hoped that she would understand.

She did. She went to the dresser and took half a dozen eggs from a basket. The man muttered something, to which she replied in one quick, sharp-sounding word. Chalky took the eggs and stowed them carefully in his inside pockets; and she produced bread, a long, crusty French loaf, which she broke in half, pressing one portion upon him. This, too, he tucked into the front of his jacket. He made a drinking motion, and the woman filled a tumbler with fresh milk, which he drank down greedily. She took the tumbler from him and, reaching out her hand, plucked timidly at his wings, his New Zealand flashes, the stripes and the brass crown on his sleeve.

"Découpez-les," she advised. She produced a pair of scissors, he cut off the badges, and removed the crown from his sleeve. He cut off his epaulettes, too, and his breast pockets, in an attempt to disguise his uniform. Then he slipped the scissors into his pocket as unobtrusively as he could, intending, when he got back to his stack, to operate on his toenails; but the woman and the man both kept pointing at his pocket, and he apologised and gave the scissors up.

The woman pushed him towards the door.

"Allez-y," she said.

He resisted slightly.

"I need somewhere to hide," he said. "The Germans —"

She shook her head.

"Le Boche," she said emphatically. *"Trop dangereux. Cachez-vous!"* She added, looking at him wide-eyed: *"J'ai peur."* She was trembling, he now saw, and he reminded himself again that she had, that very morning, had her home invaded by searching Huns, so he no longer resisted when she pushed a little harder, then stepped around him and opened the door. He stood aside, and she peered out.

"Rien," she said. *"Il n'y a personne. Allez — vite!"*

There was no mistaking her meaning, nor failing to recognise her fear. Chalky came to the door. He paused briefly, touched her arm, looked at the man, who remained standing by the dresser, and said, "Thank you very much." A vague recollection of schoolboy French came to him.

"Merci beaucoup, Madame," he said.

He stepped outside, cast a quick look about the vicinity, and raced across the wheatfield. As he reached the stack, he looked back and saw her standing within the doorway, watching him. Even as he looked, she shut the door. Chalky, on a sudden decision, did not climb onto the stack, but moved quickly on, darting from stook to stook until at last he came to a shallow depression in the ground, overgrown with grass, right at the edge of the wood. If the woman called the Germans, he would see them entering the field, and he would have some chance of slipping away unseen.

No one appeared to have seen him. The sun had, in any case, gone down some time before, and dusk was spreading across the fields.

Chalky did not actually distrust the people in the farmhouse, though he had noticed a decided lack of warmth in the man's demeanour. He thought that they would be reluctant to turn him in, having committed themselves somewhat by giving him food and advice. But it was best to be on the safe side.

After a few more minutes of tense listening, he heaved a sigh, leaned back comfortably in the sweet-scented grass, and brought out his new store of food. The eggs were raw, but to a man so powerfully hungry, that was a mere detail. He punctured the small ends one by one and sucked out the contents; and he broke chunks from the bread and ate them between draughts of liquid albumen and salty-tasting yoke. A meal fit for a king, Chalky thought. The only trouble was, there wasn't enough of it.

So he waited until about seven-thirty, lying on his back in the grass, gazing up at the stars as they appeared and brightened in the darkening sky. And presently he sat up, looked about, and selected another wheat stack in which to spend the night.

There was something of a chill in the air, as if the general air-flow — it wasn't so positive as a breeze — had shifted to the north, and he realised that he was probably in for a cold night. He was also, he admitted to himself, still hungry, not with the debilitating, demoralising emptiness which had earlier driven him to that farmhouse, but nevertheless with a nagging desire for food, which would probably deprive him of sleep. And he needed sleep, if he were to remain alert enough to outwit the Germans. So he left his hollow and set off towards another farmhouse.

Here they invited him in, gave him eggs, cooked, this time, and bread with salty farm butter, and some of the good, strong cider of Normandy; it put new heart into him. But the householder and his wife were obviously badly frightened, so he thanked them, smiled at them, patted their shoulders reassuringly, let himself out with every visible sign of caution, and went back to his wheatfield, where he burrowed beneath his selected wheat stack and slept, reasonably warm.

The next morning, he began what he thought of as his "house-to-house canvass" early. He knew that he was less likely to be caught if he waited until nightfall, but the prospect of a day's inactivity appalled him. Chalky White was not used to inactivity. You became inactive when you were dead. Therefore, in Chalky's system of logic, inactivity itself was a kind of death. Moreover, remaining concealed beneath the wheatstack, while it was as good a place of concealment as he was likely to find, meant that he could not relieve the tedium with a smoke; so off he went at sunrise to this third house, where once again he was given food and invited to leave quickly. Monsieur here was more voluble on the subject than the men of either of the other two houses. He rushed away, around the corner of the house, and returned with a leafy branch, which he held and waved over his head. It was, Chalky later discovered, a universal sign meaning "Germans near — hide in the woods quickly!" But they also managed to convey, by signs, that he should return that night, when they would have more food ready for him.

He therefore went back across the field, not to his wheatstack this time, but, following the Frenchman's suggestion, to the wood. He figured that since the Germans had searched this area, they were bound to have combed the wood thoroughly, and would be unlikely to return to it. Of course, in the wood he would be able to stretch his legs from time to time, have an occasional smoke, and it would be much more pleasant all round. Quite cheerful at the prospect, he left the field and walked for perhaps twenty yards into the wood.

He was right. It *was* pleasanter. Although early autumn, there was still a lingering summer warmth in the daytime air, and the leaves, though turning, had not yet reached their full autumnal colour, or even started to fall in earnest. The trees were still in almost full summer leaf.

Chalky began to wonder about the local peasantry. They had given him food, certainly, but they seemed to be very frightened. Chalky was well aware that they could expect severe punishment for helping an escaping prisoner-of-war. Most likely they would be shot, if caught. Yet what he had seen of the German soldiery hereabouts hardly suggested a Gestapo-like policy of rigorous harassment or brutality. Those boys were just — soldiers. They seemed to go about the tasks of occupation with about the same degree of enthusiasm as he would have expected of Allied troops. He would have been prepared to discover that most of them were not Hollywood-style rabid Nazis. Oh, they could be rough enough, no doubt. Germans, as he had observed, were apt to shout and bluster a bit. But he suspected that all most of them wanted was as soft a billet as they could contrive, with enough spare time and enough money in their pockets to make it with the local popsies; but that since there was so little love lost between French and Germans, their success rate in that field was probably not very high. So, they were very likely bored, a bit homesick, a bit disillusioned about the fruits of victory, and not a little fed up with the whole business. This would account for the general sloppiness of their search procedures. So why should the peasants be so jittery whenever Chalky showed up? Were there, perhaps, Gestapo in the area? Even while he mused upon this, the reason for their nervousness was about to become apparent.

There was a sudden long-drawn growl in Chalky's ears, growing quickly to a roaring crescendo, the unmistakeable din of American Pratt & Whitney radial engines. All at once they were right overhead at treetop height, two American Thunderbolts belting hell-for-leather across the landscape with a couple of FW190s snarling in hot pursuit. And the wood exploded with the woof-woof-woof of a German flak battery, concealed, like Chalky himself, in this very wood — this not overlarge wood! No wonder the local householders were nervous about a British airman in full uniform sauntering across their fields and knocking on their doors in broad daylight.

Chalky moved as far as he could from the sound of the guns, and burrowed earnestly into the leafiest patch of undergrowth that he could find.

And then it began to rain.

How it rained! The downpour went on and on, hour after unremitting hour. And Chalky, like any good outdoor Kiwi, built himself a maimai, and crouched in it.

The word "maimai," one understands, is of Australian origin, though at least one authority suggests that it has its roots in the Maori words for "token," in the sense of "something that represents." And Chalky would probably have gone along with that theory right then. His lean-to screen of leafy branches against the trunk of a tree bore some resemblance to a small hut. It represented an attempt to take shelter from the rain. But that was about as far as it was prepared to go. The heavy, persistant downpour found its way into the maimai at a dozen points, all of which Chalky did his best to patch. But the water, as water inevitably will, found its way around the edges of the patches, as well as finding new points of entry, until it seemed to Chalky that he was sitting in a showerbath, with the water concentrated in greater density than that of the natural fall of rain. It was as if the roof of the maimai were a funnel, collecting the rainfall over a wide area and pouring it as from a tap, onto his head, down into his collar, soaking through the thick serge of his battledress until, convinced at last that it was wetter within the maimai than it was out in the rain, Chalky scrambled out of it, stood and kicked it down. His anger now began to surface again. He began to remember old resentments, such as the time in Queensland, when the union shop steward of the gang he was shearing with called a stop-work meeting one hot afternoon when there was a race meeting at the nearest town, and declared the sheep wet —

in a region which had known no rain for nine years. He wished heartily that the man was here.

Anyway, it was getting dark again, so he mooched morosely out of the wood, shoulders hunched against the rain, hands in pockets, his hair hanging down over his forehead in trickling strands, and walked through the downpour to the friendly farmhouse.

Madame had prepared food for him, and he thanked her in his excruciating schoolboy French, which made her smile. He received nervous smiles from the whole family as he shook hands. Then he left. He took to the road, trudging through the rain, hands in pockets, splashing through the road's puddles, the water soaking through the soft leather of his flying boots; and as he walked, he thought angry, uncomplimentary thoughts about Germans. Presently he crossed the Yvetot-Havre railway, and at last, well clear of the wood and its general vicinity, and the frightened people in the farmhouses, he came upon a roadside shed in which he found an ancient and obviously long disused car. There was also a bitch of indeterminate ancestry and her litter of pups in the shed; he spoke softly and gently to the suspicious mother, allowing her to sniff his hand, stroking her, fondling her ears, carefully handling the pups. Then he lifted the whole family into the back seat of the car, and snuggled them down close to him for warmth, deciding that it was worth the risk of picking up a flea or two.

Early in the morning, with some reluctance because he was tired and wet and his ingrown toenails hurt, Chalky set out once more, still keeping to the road because the fields were sodden, and the long grass would have kept him wet to the knees. Anyway, it seemed to be a quiet, relatively unfrequented country road, and certainly made for easier walking, for all its puddled ruts.

He was hungry again, and he felt that he really needed to do something about his appearance, which the old car's mirror had told him, was worse than merely scruffy. He looked like Public Enemy Number One. So he would knock on the first door he came to, and ask for food, a beret and a pair of boots; and he must have a shave. That was of paramount importance,

Chalky figured. It wasn't merely a matter of morale or comfort, and certainly not of respectability. The thing was, German patrols would be looking for an unshaven man. It would be a clear sign that he was a fugitive.

The first door that he found was at the edge of a tiny hamlet straggling along one of the network of roads and lanes south of the main Le Havre-Rouen highway, on the edge of the Caux Plateau. The door was opened by a small boy, perhaps ten or eleven years old, skinny and sparrow-like as so many French kids seemed to be, buttoned up in clothes half a size too small. But this boy was unreservedly on Chalky's side. Where his parents were, Chalky never knew, but it didn't seem to matter. What mattered, what came to matter increasingly as Chalky's odyssey progressed, was that you could always count on the kids. He was sure that they were every bit as aware of the danger as their parents, but they were alert and spry and gallant, with a contempt for the Germans which, in an adult, might have been suicidal, and they seemed to relish the risk. It was all a big game of cops and robbers, to them, and they were very, very good at it. This boy, cautioning Chalky to be quiet, gave him bread, cheese, the inevitable eggs, and — glory be! — a beret. Boots, unluckily, were another matter. So few Frenchmen seemed to take size eleven. With sore feet but renewed confidence, Chalky took to the road again, striding out briskly, grateful for the warmth which returned to his chilled body.

He walked on, seeing the odd peasant working head down in his fields, totally engrossed, evidently not seeing, perhaps not wanting to see, what was going on in the world beyond his own fields. But there were no Germans, nor even so much as a car or a truck on the road. As the sun climbed over the sky, his clothing dried on his body.

That day, he knocked on one more door, and again his frantic miming won him food and, more importantly, a shave, which redoubled his self-confidence. He had no illusions regarding his chances of absolute avoidance of German patrols, but shaven recently, and with his beret on his head, his hands in his pockets, and moving at a peasant's bent-backed shuffle, he felt that he could pass muster.

His anger had subsided at the time of his meeting with the boy, and this second piece of good fortune had increased his confidence immeasurably. At this time, the thing began to assume the aspect of a sporting contest. The home team was out to block his every move. He couldn't outrun them all, but he could fool them with his ducking and dodging. He believed that he was more intelligent than they were. And in his new mood of optimism, he was able to tell himself that he had one priceless advantage. They were many, they were almost everywhere. All that meant was that they were highly visible. He, on the other hand, was one man, barely noticeable. They had to guess at his intentions, try to cover a hundred possible moves he might make, but he could see them, what they were doing, and he didn't have to guess. To catch him, they needed luck. To avoid them, he needed only caution. They were an organisation — patrols, platoons, companies, battalions. They had to arrange and plan and co-ordinate. He could act on the spur of the moment, as the circumstances dictated, without reference to anyone else. They had to be clever, and their showing to date in that respect had not been anything to write home about. He had only to be careful. And once he got to Paris, became one anonymous body in a huge, close-packed population, he reckoned that they would have lost him altogether. He doubted if they would still even be looking. Most likely, for them, he would have ceased to exist.

Strangely, it never occurred to him that there might be other evading airmen dodging about the Normandy countryside. For the time being he had forgotten that other damaged Spitfire that the four FW190s had peeled off to attack. This whole setup was his problem. He was on his own. The Germans he saw were looking for him in particular; that he did not for a moment doubt. The factors in this question were Chalky White and the German Army. And, possibly, the Gestapo.

Chalky's confidence was thus at a reasonably high level.

Even so, he knew well enough that it was foolhardy to take undue risks — and road-walking in broad daylight was risky. So eventually, while it was still high noon, he left the road and moved into an overgrown, grassy field, where he lay down in a dip in the ground and began to eat his lunch.

His timing was fortuitously perfect, because within moments of his settling comfortably in the grassy hollow, there began what seemed to be an endless procession of horse-and-trap patrols — a trap containing two Germans, one driving, one with weapon at the ready — scout cars, sections on foot and in trucks, passing along the road in monotonous procession. It was not monotonous at first, naturally. Chalky lay for perhaps the first half hour, pressed against the damp ground, from time to time peering cautiously between the grassy stems, watching, until he felt a sudden stab of fear that his face might be spotted. Then he would thrust his face down, hiding it in the crook of an arm, until curiosity made him take another cautious look. For a time, his earlier confidence evaporated, and their very numbers seemed to underline the fact that the real odds were very uneven indeed — the entire German army against Chalky White.

He was profoundly glad when, at dusk, the last German activity ceased, and he could go to the farmhouse he had seen a couple of hundred yards up the road.

The farmer himself answered Chalky's knocking. He was a surly fellow, with deep-set, shifty eyes, and Chalky found himself wishing fervently that he could speak French, because it was difficult to explain in sign language something as abstract as "Please don't bother." And he couldn't bring himself to simply walk off when the farmer began putting on his coat, and talking to him, and making it plain that he was anxious to help.

At least, that was what Chalky hoped that the man was proposing. The pats on the shoulder that were meant to be reassuring weren't, and the shark-smile that failed to reach the sunken eyes seemed far more menacing than snarls or threats.

Far from happy about it, Chalky agreed to go with the man.

They set out in the gathering darkness, back down the road along which the patrols had gone, and along a branching lane which led between copses, with which the countryside hereabouts was liberally dotted. So far, so good — but when the lane debouched onto a wider road, Chalky saw orderly rows of huts, and small pinpoints of light from obscured bulbs, all spread across a humped field, with a sentry box on the roadside, not a hundred yards from the lane. It seemed he was about to be betrayed.

In a savage instant, he wished he had his revolver. His instinct warned him not to indulge himself by giving the man a thumping in August that he would remember with pain when the snows were on the hills; for though the peasant was not as tall as he, he was thickset, with legs like tree trunks, and gnarled, massive hands which had obviously known years of manual labour. Doubtless he also possessed a good set of lungs. While Chalky had no doubt that he could clobber the fellow, he would probably be faced with sufficient resistance to delay his own departure, and his presence would be heralded with enough noise to waken the dead — and the entire German detachment.

Without warning, Chalky suddenly ran from the lane, into the trees. The startled collaborator took a couple of hestitant steps after him, but evidently thought better of it. It is probable that he went to the German camp to rouse a pursuit. Chalky never knew for certain. He plunged on, through clinging undergrowth and sapling thickets, out into the open fields at last, gasping for breath, sweat pouring from every pore, a painful stitch in his side, and his toes, his agonising, tortured toes shooting fiery darts through his feet, until he came upon another gritty, dusty country lane. Exhausted and hungry, he hadn't the heart for another confrontation, so he knocked on no more doors that night, but found shelter in an empty stable, where he covered himself with what mouldy straw he could gather together, and slept.

He awoke at sunup, and was about to leave the stable when he heard trucks of some kind on the nearby road. He had been sleeping in a stall, on some old chaff bags, and he stood up and moved to a cobwebby window. The surrounding fields were alive with searching Germans, and even as he watched, footsteps sounded in the stable yard. He dived for a dark corner, behind an old farm dray; an obvious hiding place, but there was no time to seek a better one. He crouched in the corner, covering himself as well as he could with sacks and straw as the footsteps sounded in the doorway. Peering from his hiding place, he saw a Frenchman come in and cast penetrating glances about the interior.

German commands and the heavy footfalls of jackbooted soldiery were coming closer. Turning his head, Chalky could see them through cracks in the stable's dilapidated timbers. He looked again at the Frenchman, who suddenly stared straight at him, hard. It was impossible to tell whether he had seen him or not. But suddenly, the Frenchman turned, walked to the stable door, started in a somewhat stagey fashion, and ran out and away. The Germans took off after him like hounds after a hare.

It was possible that they were looking for the Frenchman, Chalky thought later, or that the Frenchman thought they were. But he didn't think so. He was inclined to believe that the peasant had spotted him, and had decoyed the Germans away. It seemed likely. These Norman peasants had that kind of cunning. Even so, it was a brave thing to do. Some trigger-happy German might easily have shot him, and if, as they probably did, they caught him, he would have had to undergo, at the very least, one of their blustering interrogations.

Chalky left the stable as soon as he conveniently could. The decoy had led the Germans off, which suggested that they had indeed caught him, and had taken him for interrogation. At all events there was, once more, a clear road ahead of him, without a Hun in sight. The day was still quite young. His watch told him that it was barely nine-thirty.

Oddly, in spite of his narrow escape, he began to feel safer. The day was warm, and the road ran between six-foot embankments crowned with beech trees. He was on a narrowing escarpment, with the gleam of the River Seine glimpsed through trees far to his right, whenever he scrambled to the top of the embankment to look around and get his bearings. Inclining away to his left, with the road turning down towards it, was a pleasant valley, where the farmsteads were like green oases behind their sheltering, tree-topped embankments; pleasant, half-timbered houses sitting in the midst of their apple orchards, with oaks and elms and beeches shading them and their clusters of outbuildings. Tethered cattle browsed over the green grass, and woods patched the valley sides. There were fields that were grain-golden, or green with late vegetables. It was all pleasantly reassuring, conveying as it did the feeling that nothing had happened to disturb these storybook farms, and that all was going on as it had always gone on, and always would go on. And in his grimy, tattered uniform and his beret, he fitted in with those surroundings, he felt. He was in harmony with them, one more earthy, bent-backed farm labourer.

Feeling more confident, Chalky stopped walking. The sense of desperate urgency seemed suddenly to have left him. His toes were still giving him trouble, and it was sheer relief just to stand still for a while on the grassy verge, twisting his feet so that he stood on the outer edges of his soles, sparing his toes contact with the boots for a little while.

The road now ran as straight as an arrow, down into the valley, for about a quarter of a mile. Then it twisted off to the right, disappearing behind the tree-crowned embankment. Far off to his right front was a village; and beyond the village, on the gently sloping valley side, stood an old, grey chateau, a building of massive but pleasant dignity, set amongst and rising above a pride of elms and oaks and beeches, which shaded its park. Looking at it, Chalky knew what he had to do.

He was, he acknowledged at last, desperately lonely and, in spite of his confidence in his own ability to see this thing through, not a little scared. It was bad enough having to screw up his courage again and again to knock on doors and beg, not knowing whether the house he approached might be billeting Germans, or whether its rightful inhabitants were friendly. But it was the frustrating pantomine of trying to make his needs understood by signs that was worst of all. If only he could speak some French. If only he had someone, some companion, with whom he could converse in English.

Well, the hell with it. What he ought to do, what he probably should have done in the first place, was to hunt up the biggest, wealthiest-looking house he could find; because its owners, being people of wealth, would presumably also be people of culture, bound to have a spare language or two up their sleeves, one of which would almost certainly be English. And there, across the valley, was just such a house. He would go to it and ask for help, all the things he needed, including a pair of size eleven boots.

He felt better for having come to this decision. Right or wrong, at least he was moving with purpose again, instead of dodging erractically along unknown roads.

He stepped out onto the road and began to stride down it, heedless, for the first few paces, of his sore toes; and even when they forced themselves upon his attention and made him limp, he still swung his arms and walked straight-backed and jaunty, and even began to whistle.

Around the corner ahead of him, the road would point him straight towards the chateau, he reckoned. It would be there, in front of him, beckoning him on.

Around the corner ahead of him, coming towards him, rode a pair of German soldiers on bicycles....

4.

The Germans rode their bicycles as they seemed to do everything of what might be termed a "parade" or "duty" nature — with a sort of wooden precision. The shock of fear that tore through Chalky as they came around that corner froze him into — not immobility, but a sort of guilty hesitancy, which was almost immediately damped down by that impression of mechanical rigidity. These characters, he noticed, continued to sit bolt upright in their saddles, eyes to the front, pedalling in unison. Except for the coal-scuttle helmets and the rifles across their backs at identical angles, they could have been a couple of country curates going about their parochial business. It didn't, of course, mean that they hadn't noticed him, Chalky thought, or recognised him for what he was. But these characters, these conquerors, he told himself sourly, probably expected that their very presence would freeze lesser creatures into instant immobility and obedience. That was the way their world was. They expected it as surely as they expected the law of gravity to work without exception. He would freeze — or he would run. If he froze, they would ride up to him and start shouting for his papers, his name, his account of himself. Or he could run — and they would step from their cycles with that mechanical precision, and one would stand, and one would kneel and they would aim their rifles carefully and, practically by numbers, would shoot him down.

Unless —.

If a soldier saw something lying on the parade ground, he

reacted to it in one of two ways. Either he reacted to it as the situation and the drillbook called for, or he didn't see it at all, depending on whether or not the object was a fixture. So, in Chalky's system of logic, it followed that the best way of avoiding the unwelcome attentions of these Huns was to appear to be a fixture, part of the scenery, an item of entirely reasonable furniture. The episodes of the rain barrel and the wheat stack bore that out.

He forced himself to keep shuffling towards them — they were still fifty yards distant — with his shoulders stooped and his face downturned. But his eyes searched the ground on either side of the road. Where he was at the moment, there was no roadside embankment, but a straggle of unwilling gorse bushes, not quite coherent enough to be called a hedge, and beyond that, on the edge of a newly ploughed field, stood a plough.

Chalky, hands now in pockets, back bowed, beret on head, shuffled over, bent, and began to fiddle with it industriously, giving it his entire attention. He was, in those moments, a farm labourer working on a plough in a field, an item of entirely reasonable furniture, part of the landscape.

The bicycle patrol pedalled past him, neither German giving him so much as an incurious glance. He waited until they had disappeared round a bend and were screened by a tree-crowned dyke. Then he straightened up, heaved a sigh of huge relief and resumed his walk, making for the chateau.

As he turned the corner around which the Germans had appeared, he saw in front of him a church tower and a smattering of roofs above the treetops, a little way up the far side of the valley, where it lifted up to the Caux Plateau. Still edgy after his experience with the cycle patrol, he felt unhappy at the prospect of walking through a village in broad daylight. Probably there would be Huns billeted there — they seemed to be everywhere, infesting the countryside like a plague of mice — and it would be immediately apparent to them that he was a stranger. Then, of course, there would be questions. So he approached the village warily, looking about him for a possible detour that would allow him to bypass the place. It was with considerable relief, therefore, that he found a road to the chateau branching off about a quarter of a mile before the village (now identified as Touffreville-la-Corbeline). He turned into the chateau road with gratitude, because its embankments promptly hid him from the now plain-to-be-seen village street.

Soon he came upon a monumentally huge gateway shaded by colossal elms. He walked through it and up the curving carriageway beneath magnificent shade trees. Suddenly, before him, across a circular lawn, stood the chateau, old, grey, mellow, and benignly imposing; not an ostentatious frivolity from the days of the French kings, but a country squire of a building, solid and square and sensible, with broad, welcoming steps leading up to the first floor. And on those sweeping front steps stood a woman and four men.

There was something unreal about it. Up until now, everything had been foreign — foreign houses, foreign language, foreign clothes, a foreign way of doing things; but here was something touchingly familiar and home-like, as understandable as a cup of afternoon tea. The lady of the house had obviously been entertaining, and was now seeing her guests off, exactly as Chalky's mother often had, on the front steps of her own home, with a final pleasant exchange of thanks and farewells. Almost, Chalky forgot the grandeur of the house. He stood there in the shade of those immemorial oaks and elms, watching, entranced. But soon the very size and consequence of the house insinuated its way quietly but impressively upon his attention, reminding him of where he was and who he was and why he was here. He took a deep breath, adjusted his features into a smile he didn't really feel, and walked forward, out of the shade, into the bright evening sunlight, outwardly far more confident than he felt.

They turned, all five of them, and returned his stare but not his grin. It must be all right, he kept telling himself. There are no German uniforms amongst them, no stiff military shoulders. They are all respectably dressed, reasonably relaxed civilians. There was a watchfulness in their eyes, but no obvious hostility, as far as he could see.

He walked up to the steps and began to mount them, fancying as he did so that there was a quick quirk of disapproval on one man's face, but only a well-bred passiveness in the

The "very small boy" on his pony, Nothing Nicer.

The "brand new pilot," Sgt. L.S.M. White, after gaining his wings…

. . . and the "pugnacious-looking, bulbous-nosed Cessna Crane" on which he won them.

"A Spitfire was what he wanted to fly . . ." Chalky White in the cockpit of a Spitfire 5b, with which 485 Squadron was equipped before receiving the Mk. 9b.

expressions of the other three, and a faint flicker of — was it amusement? — about Madame's mouth and eyes.

He had abandoned his peasant shuffle a few paces from the foot of the steps, and now advanced straight-backed, with well-held shoulders, and his head up. He was no longer a French farm labourer, but Flight-Sergeant L.S.M. White of 485 Squadron, Royal Air Force.

No one said a word as he climbed the steps. He halted a step or two below them, looking at each in turn, wondering how to begin, how to break that slightly strained silence.

"Does anyone here speak English?" he asked at last.

There was an almost embarrassed pause. The men looked at each other, and then, with one accord, at Madame.

"I speak English," she said. Her tone was gentle, her accent almost that of Mayfair or Park Lane. She didn't actually smile, Chalky noticed, and neither did any of the men, but her face retained its pleasant calm. She volunteered no further information, but inclined her head slightly, waiting. The conversational ball, it seemed, was fairly back in Chalky's court.

"I'm RAF," Chalky said. "I need help."

The woman looked at him, still with that benign expression. At last she said, "Yes, we'd heard there was an escaped British airman in the vicinity."

Again she waited, saying no more, clearly not about to commit herself, but willing to, as it were, examine his credentials.

He dipped into his pocket, but one of the men made a restless movement, as if trying to catch her eye, and she made a small, arresting motion with her hand. Chalky kept his hand in his pocket, clutching his wings, while she turned to her guests.

"Mes chers amis," she said, *"merci pour le plaisir de cette visite. Docteur, à demain. Abbé, messieurs —."*

They bowed, and walked down the steps. The Vicar, Chalky surmised, and the local Nobs.

Near the foot of the steps, they turned like a small chorus line, and bowed again to Madame. Chalky thought that M'sieu' le Docteur almost winked at him, a barely perceptible flutter of his right eyelid, accompanied by the faintest shadow of a smile. Then they turned and walked away together.

Madame looked at Chalky. "RAF?" she prompted gently.

He fumbled into his pocket, around his grimy handkerchief, which he did not want her to see, because grimy handkerchiefs and this gracious lady didn't seem to belong together. He got his flashes and his wings together in his big fist, and hauled them out and showed them to her.

Madame seemed barely to glance at them. Her eyes were turned down at his feet, as if she were weighing him up in her mind, him and his flimsy credentials. Then, quite suddenly, she smiled at Chalky.

"You had better come inside," she said, and turned and led the way.

Inside, Chalky said apologetically: "I'm a bit of a nuisance. I'm sorry. It's just that I —"

"You are not a nuisance in the least," she said. "I'm very glad you came to us."

"You'll be taking an awful risk," Chalky warned.

"No," she said, shaking her head. "I might have been, except that I assured myself that you are — what you say you are. One has to be careful, you understand. The Germans are not above trying to discover our attitudes by posing as airmen in distress. But — you have your credentials, your wings, and the badges with eagles and 'New Zealand' on them."

After the liberation, Madame, whose name was Duhamel, wrote to Chalky's mother:

I suppose he told you how he came, at the end of a beautiful day, all clad in his uniform, in front of our chateau, asking me, "Do you speak English?" I must say that I was amazed, for at that time we were surrounded by German soldiers, and it was the first time since four years that I had heard this dear language. I trusted him immediately, though we had been told to be careful, many German spies clad in British uniform visiting French families to know their feelings towards the Allied armies — but I knew on the spot that this big boy could not be other than honest and fair. . .

And that, even allowing for the fact that it was Chalky's mother she was writing to, was undoubtedly true. But she also told Chalky that the clincher had been the English lolly paper which fell from his pocket onto the steps when he fished out his wings and eagles.

In any case, they hit it off famously, Chalky White from the Waikaka Valley, and Monsieur and Madame Duhamel of the Chateau, Touffreville. Madame gave him a glass of wine and some food, and while he ate, he told her something of himself, and she listened with polite attention.

"My name," he said, "is White, Leslie White; but everybody calls me Chalky," he added quickly. He didn't feel at home with anything that smacked of stiff formality.

"Ah, yes," Madame Duhamel said, "the nickname. Nicknames are very English."

"Oh, I'm not English," he reminded her. "At least, not born-in-England English."

"New Zealand," she responded, nodding. "I do not know New Zealand, very much, but a little, from school, you understand. And there were New Zealand men in France in the last war, I remember."

"I'm from the South Island," Chalky said. It felt good to say it, to feel that it meant something to someone. Somehow that made it meaningful again for him, almost as if he could go back to it at will. "We farm in the Waikaka Valley. That's in South Otago, almost in Southland, right down near the bottom of the South Island."

"So far from home," she murmured sadly. Then, brightening, she declared: "For now, you have a home! This is your home!"

"Bravo!" A man's voice spoke from the doorway behind Chalky, and he looked around and stood up. The man advancing into the room with hand outstretched was a pleasant-looking fellow. From his appearance, his well-pressed slacks, the cravat about his neck under the open shirt collar, his fresh, clean-shaven complexion, Chalky surmised that he was the lord of the manor, Madame's husband.

He shook Chalky's hand warmly, then waved him back into his chair.

"I interrupt your meal," he said. "Forgive me." His English was slightly more heavily accented than Madame's, though it was a long way from Maurice Chevalier or most of the pilots of 341 (French) Squadron with whom Chalky had set out — was it only five days ago?

"I don't want to be a nuisance," Chalky said. "If you could just —"

"A nuisance? A nuisance? Of course you are not a nuisance," Monsieur Duhamel declared stoutly.

"My husband, Monsieur Duhamel," Madame Duhamel introduced, belatedly and unnecessarily.

"Pleased to meet you," Chalky acknowledged.

"We will help you," Monsieur Duhamel promised, "of course. But we must be — circumspect, my friend."

"This is Leslie White, of New Zealand," Madame Duhamel told her husband, determined to complete the introductions. "His friends call him Chalky. Chalky White. Is it not amusing?"

"Most," Monsieur agreed gravely. "If we may be your friends? I shall name you Chalky."

"Bang on," Chalky agreed.

"Now, how are we going to assist you?" Monsieur Duhamel wondered. The question did not really require an answer, Chalky perceived. Monsieur Duhamel was merely thinking aloud.

"Somewhere to conceal him," Madame Duhamel suggested.

"Yes," Monsieur agreed, and smiled at her. They could, Chalky thought, have been discussing something pleasantly domestic, like bottling gooseberries, or deciding on the colour of the new bedroom curtains, rather than a matter which could well mean the firing squad or concentration camp for both of them. To Chalky, Monsieur said, still in that same matter-of-fact tone:

"I am devastated that we cannot keep you in the house, but you must understand, the other half of the chateau is occupied by Germans."

Chalky, with his fork half way to his mouth, stopped, shocked.

Monsieur sounded as if it were merely a matter for mild regret, a trifling inconvenience, and that somehow took a lot of the kick out of what, for Chalky, was still a shockingly demoralising piece of intelligence. Germans, in the same house!

"The cottage —," Madame Duhamel mentioned.

"But of course! Godefroi will help; and it is perfectly safe," Monsieur Duhamel said, taking up the suggestion enthusiastically. "Chalky, when you have finished your meal — and please do not hurry yourself unnecessarily, for we cannot move you before dark — I will fetch Godefroi, and he will take you to his cottage."

The sun had gone down an hour before, and a glance at the windows showed Chalky that twilight was already deepening.

"Godefroi?" he asked hesitantly.

"Godefroi works on the estate," Monsieur Duhamel explained. "He and his wife and family occupy the cottage. Oh, do not trouble yourself. It is perfectly safe. The Germans have no reason to go up there, and in any case, the officers have had the goodness to discourage their men from wandering over the property at will."

"And there," Madame said with housewifely practicality, "you shall have a hot bath, and a comfortable bed to sleep in. Madame, Godefroi's wife, will give you a hot meal —"

"I could do with both," Chalky agreed, "and a shave. Oh, and a pair of boots, if that's possible. These flying boots —" he stuck out a foot " — aren't too good for walking in."

"Ah, yes," Monsieur Duhamel said. "We shall see what may be obtained."

"Size eleven," Chalky told him. Monsieur Duhamel pursed his lips and nodded slowly.

And then, for a little while, having finished eating, Chalky sat on the sofa and talked to Madame, while Monsieur went away to fetch Godefroi and to warn Godefroi's wife. Chalky talked to Madame about home, about his mother, about shearing in outback Australia, and, perhaps more than he had ever before found words for, the free, wind-blown, slightly unkempt beauty of his native hills, the willow-lined creeks, hillsides furred with tussock that flattened in wheals before the singing wind, like the pelt on the flanks of the red deer that roamed the mountains, the harrier hawks, the Blue

Mountains, the great, calm lakes to the west, and the friendly rivers. Madame listened, and asked him about his family, so that it was all the very next best thing to a visit at home itself.

Then Monsieur Duhamel returned, bringing with him a gnarled, lean man with a complexion like a well-worn tan shoe, and a shrewd, blue, peasant's eye.

"This," Monsieur said, "is Godefroi. He is one of our men, and is faithful and always to be trusted. And he dislikes Germans."

Godefroi's expression did not change, either to show embarrassment or to confirm Monsieur's assertions. Chalky took it as a sign that he neither spoke nor understood English.

"Godefroi will take you to the cottage," Monsieur Duhamel told Chalky.

"If there are Germans about —" Chalky demurred.

"Do not be concerned," Monsieur Duhamel said. "The men frequently come to the house for instructions at the end of the day. And it is getting quite dark."

With Godefroi, Chalky left the house by a back door, walking along paths which squared off the kitchen garden plots, through the orchard and out into the fields by way of a small gate in a hedge.

Godefroi's cottage was a pretty home, thatched and half-timbered, though Chalky could not see these details very well in the dark. Godefroi ushered him into the large kitchen, and as they entered, the peasant said, in heavily accented English: "'Ere you will conceal yourself. You will be safe, 'ere."

Chalky looked about him. The room itself was spacious, though much of the space was taken up by a dresser, and cupboards and a large deal table, the homely furniture of a farmhouse. Near the table, Godefroi's wife stood, her arms lightly embracing two children, about nine and eleven years of age. She looked at Chalky a little apprehensively.

'G'day," Chalky said cheerfully.

The children did not respond, but looked at him wide-eyed.

"*Bon soir,*" the woman said uncertainly.

"*Bon soir,*" Chalky responded, and smiled at her. She did not return his smile, and seemed to be a little afraid. Godefroi said something to her in French, in which Chalky caught the words *aviateur anglais.* Madame smiled, then, a nervous twitching of the corners of her mouth. She conducted Chalky up a narrow stair, to a bedroom, a cheerfully chintzy room which boasted an iron bedstead with clean sheets and a patchwork quilt. He nodded happy approval.

"That's terrific, Madame," he acknowledged enthusiastically, and received a brighter, more self-assured smile.

Godefroi stood in the doorway.

"Do not, for any — *raison* move about outside the 'ouse," he said, "unless it to visit the... *la toilette* ...how do you say?"

"The privy?" Chalky suggested.

"*Oui. La ...preevy,* ha ha. You are to 'ave a... a bath, now, M'sieu', and then you will eat with us 'ot food." He turned in the doorway and pointed to the stairs. "The bath is down, in the back of the 'ouse. Madame, she will show."

"Thanks," Chalky said. "A bath'll be great."

As he moved towards the door, Godefroi stood aside, then stepped in behind him and followed him down the stairs. At the foot of the staircase, he said: "What work do you do?"

"I'm a fighter pilot," Chalky said.

Godefroi frowned, and shook his head.

"Before this," he said.

"You mean, at home?"

"*Oui.* At home."

"I'm a farmer," Chalky confided.

"Ah." Godefroi's eyes smiled. Chalky felt now that he was truly accepted.

Monsieur and Madame Duhamel came to Chalky that night, bringing a French Army canvas bag. They found him relaxed, warm with food and cider, sipping Calvados, talking to the half-comprehending Godefroi about farms of two and three thousand acres, with flocks numbering thousands, woolsheds where the shearers used machine clippers, where there were six stands, all working at once, with each shearer putting through hundreds in a day, and sheepruns in outback Australia which were the size of Normandy.

He stood up as the Duhamels came in. Madame Duhamel

opened the bag on the kitchen table and brought forth a pair of Monsieur Duhamel's trousers, a civilian tie, and an identity card filled in with the name, L. Blanc.

"We need a photograph," Monsieur Duhamel said.

"I've got one," Chalky told him. It was a part of the escape kit — several small photographs. He fished the oiled linen bag out of his pocket, selected a photograph, and handed it to Monsieur Duhamel, who produced a small bottle of mucilage and proceeded to affix the photograph to the card.

"Sign the identity card — so," Monsieur Duhamel said, handing Chalky a fountain pen. Chalky signed "L. Blanc" with a flourish.

"Do not, however, produce this card unless it is positively demanded," Monsieur advised.

Chalky nodded.

"I apologise," Madame Duhamel said. "No boots. There is no one on the estate who wears size eleven. So big!"

Chalky felt a pang of disappointment, but strove not to show it. Yet it must have shown, because Madame, watching his eyes intently, said:

"Perhaps, when we have made contact with certain people who can help you —"

"No." Chalky said firmly.

"No?" Monsieur's eyebrows shot up. "But, Chalky, there are organisations which —"

"No," Chalky insisted.

"But why?"

"Because —. Look, I don't want to seem ungrateful. I can't thank you enough for what you've done. But every minute I stay here, the more danger you're in, you and Madame Duhamel, and Godefroi, and his wife and children. I mean, if they catch me, I go into a prisoner-of-war camp — if they can hold me," Chalky added with a faint grin. "But if they catch you . . . ."

"They shall not," Monsieur Duhamel said positively.

"Maybe not. I hope not. But they *are* living in the same house. Look, I could never forgive myself if I got you into trouble. If I go it on my own, and I make a mistake, I've only got myself to blame, and only I have to face the consequences. Besides. . . ."

He nearly said that he had had one experience of trusting himself to someone who promised to take him to people who would help him, and who had promptly tried to hand him over to the Germans. But he realised that this would sound as if he mistrusted the Duhamels, and he really trusted them utterly.

"Besides. . . .?" Monsieur Duhamel asked.

"It's a very long walk, to Spain," Chalky said. "I'll have to get cracking if I'm to make it before the winter weather sets in."

"A few more days," Madame Duhamel said, almost pleading. "You must have rest, to build up your strength for such a journey. And, who knows? Perhaps in that time we may discover a pair of size eleven boots —"

"You're very good to me," Chalky said, "but I've got to keep going."

"Stay tonight," Madame requested. "We will look after you. You need rest. You look so... tired."

"I could do with a decent night's sleep," Chalky conceded. He nodded. "I had intended to stay the night. Thanks very much. But I must get away early."

"Where will you go?" Madame asked.

"South," Chalky said decisively. "South to Paris. Somewhere I'll catch a train."

She shook her head.

"Listen to me," she said. "Tomorrow you must go north."

"North!" But —"

"South is Caudebec-en-Caux. You pass through the village of Rançon, where there are Germans. And there are many Germans in Caudebec. It is not a large town. You would be noticeable. South-east is Rouen, with many towns and villages along the way,"

"But, north —"

"North is Yvetot. There are no Germans billeted in Touffreville at present, though their patrols come through it constantly. One of our workmen will take you through the... the *bocage* — the woods and copses around Touffreville, and set you on the main road to Yvetot. There you may catch a train for Paris, since that is what you are determined to do." She paused and looked at him. "It is a risk," she said, "but in Yvetot are no Germans quartered, and the risk is much less than walking south, I believe. The train takes an hour, perhaps, to reach Paris."

Chalky, listening to her careful English, thought that what she said made good sense. But....

"I have some money," he said, "but I'm not too familiar with your currency. What's it likely to cost me?"

"You will have enough," she said, "be assured. Wait until morning. Your guide will come, very early. He will bring you money and other necessities."

"You're very good to me," Chalky said again.

"It is easily arranged," Monsieur said deprecatingly.

"It is easily arranged," Madame repeated. She reached out suddenly and gripped his shoulders.

"Stay with us until we can arrange safe travelling," she pleaded once more.

"I can't," he told her. "It wouldn't be right. I'm very grateful to you. You and Mr Duhamel have been terrific, but if I was to get you into trouble, I don't think I'd ever be able to sleep at nights. I — I can't thank you enough for what you've done already. If you only knew how great it is, just to be able to talk with someone...."

Madame Duhamel looked at him searchingly, and he was surprised to see that her eyes were brimming. She essayed a brave smile, though two tears spilled over and ran down her cheeks.

"We are afraid for you," she said, "both I and my husband. We have no sons of our own," she added sadly. Then she smiled at him again, embraced him and left the cottage. Monsieur wrung his hand, patted him on the shoulders, and smiled.

"*Bonne chance*, Chalky," he said. Then he, too, was gone.

They were as good as their word. The promised farm workman called for him in the morning, bringing money, bread coupons and food. Chalky ate a quick breakfast of croissants and honey, and drank some cider. Then he made his bed neatly, knotted his civilian tie, put on his beret, shouldered his canvas bag, and said his goodbyes to Godefroi and his family. Then he stepped outside.

"Let's go," he said to his guide.

"Venez avec moi," the guide said, and in the chill of the early morning, beneath a cold, nacreous sky, they set off across the fields, presently coming to a track which, judging by the weeds and grass and oak seedlings which encroached upon it, was seldom used.

It was a sinuous path, and here and there the guide took shortcuts, trudging through the dew-wet grass, climbing over tree-topped embankments and coming ever and again to the overgrown track, a rutted, grassy avenue between stands of trees. The guide walked ahead. Chalky followed, about thirty yards behind.

Occasionally they would pass other peasants, early at work on their land, and the guide would give them a wave, or, rather, a perfunctory lift of his hand, while keeping his head down and his gaze apparently on the ground a yard or two ahead. When Chalky passed the same spot, he would imitate the gesture. It amused him to imagine the comments that his passing would arouse. A countryman himself, he knew all of the countryman's lively curiosity. He was accustomed to exchanging comments and speculations regarding the identity of a car passing in a cloud of dust past a country homestead, and he could imagine how these peasants would react. "That's old Gaston from the Chateau, isn't it?" "Wonder where he's going at this time of day?" "Who's that other one? That's not Godefroi, is it?" "Maybe they've got a new man at the Chateau."

At length, a kilometre to the north of Touffreville-la-Corbeline, the guide climbed to the top of another embankment and stood, waiting for Chalky to catch him up. There, at the foot of the embankment, was the main road to Yvetot.

"Suivez la route, la-bas," the guide said, pointing. Then, his dour face relaxing in a grin of surprising warmth, he seized Chalky's hand in both of his, pumped it twice, and let it go.

"Bonne chance," he said, turning and stumping away in the direction from which he had come.

Chalky looked at his retreating back for a moment, then shrugged his shoulders almost as if assuming a burden. Alone again, he went down to the road and set off towards Yvetot and, he hoped, the train for Paris.

There was no one in sight. The roadside embankments at this point hid the fields from him, and the road remained empty. It meandered, rather, up and over and around the dovetailing spurs which reached down into the valley from the Caux Plateau. The valley was not deep, so the climb out of it was gentle, and made for easy walking. Indeed, it was quite a pleasant walk. Chalky had managed to operate on his toenails, and while still uncomfortable, they were, so far, bearable. He could almost forget them, this morning. He walked upright, briskly, not troubling to assume his farm-labourer character, since there was no one near to watch him. No one, that is, until he heard the unmistakeable rattle of a bicycle on the *pavé* behind him.

It was too late to stoop into his round-shouldered peasant shuffle. To do so abruptly would excite suspicion. So he continued to swing along, marching rather than walking — and tensely awaiting the command to stop.

5.

The bicycle came closer, and Chalky fought down a desire to turn and face it. He had always been one to turn and face trouble or fears. It was part of his nature, to meet them head on. But to look around was to suggest to the patrol, or whatever it was, that he was apprehensive, and apprehension would be taken as a sign of guilt. To turn around would be to invite questioning. No, his best chance was to keep on walking, apparently unconcerned, as if he had a perfect right to be there.

The bicycle was alongside him, and then past him. Its rider was a French farm boy, perhaps fifteen years of age. He eyed Chalky curiously, which Chalky put down to that country inquisitiveness. The boy did not speak, but simply rode on.

Over the next kilometre, he came back twice. Ordinarily, Chalky might still not have thought anything of it. If it had been a kid of ten or twelve, he could have dismissed it as, simply, a boy being a boy, pedalling up the gentle slope just to enjoy the fun of freewheeling down it. But a fifteen-year-old, and especially a farm fifteen-year-old, in Chalky's experience, was rather too old for that sort of thing. Besides, the lad looked at him with frank curiosity every time he came past.

The boy came toiling up behind him for the third time, and pedalled ahead to where the road, no longer climbing, turned sharply to the left and disappeared behind the embankment. He didn't go around the corner, but stopped in the middle of the road, dismounted and bent over his bike, fiddling with the chain. After a moment, he straightened up and wheeled the machine towards the left-hand embankment, as if to clear the roadway while he made a repair. But as soon as he was at the foot of the embankment, he remounted and came riding back towards Chalky. Drawing up to him, he stopped, standing astride the bike, and said, hesitantly and with a heavy accent which rendered the words all but unintelligible:

"Are you English?"

Chalky, startled, hesitated. Then he nodded. The boy raised his arm in the now familiar branch-waving gesture, over his head, his fingers spread to represent foliage.

"Cachez!" he said, adding in the same urgent tone, *"Jairmans!"*

Chalky still stood there, and the boy said, almost frantically; *"Dans le bois, là-bas!"*

Two German trucks came around the corner, heading towards them. The boy's face became rigid and pale, but he laid a hand upon Chalky's sleeve, and they moved off the road. The trucks, to their joint-loosening relief, sped past, disappearing around a bend, heading towards Touffreville.

The boy now began to point with urgent stabbing motions and said again: *"Dans le bois, là-bas.* The... wood, there. I come back." Then he mounted his bicycle and pedalled off towards Touffreville.

Chalky hesitated no longer. He scrambled up over the embankment and down the other side, into a field of weeds and stubble, on the far side of which was a large wood, its edge ragged with clumps of gorse. He made for it in some haste.

He found a patch of undergrowth just within the wood, an uncut thicket in which he was able to conceal himself and still keep an eye on the embankment and the unkempt field.

The lad was as good as his promise — and better. In less than half an hour he was back. According to Chalky's watch, it was still quite early, a few minutes short of half-past eight, and the sun was not yet very high. The boy must live somewhere close, he figured, to have got back so soon. He might have been on his way to school at Yvetot, but Chalky did not think so, on the whole. It was, he figured, much more likely that he was simply an inquisitive farm boy who had spotted him from his home, maybe as he walked across the fields with his guide from the chateau, and had recognised him, more or less, for what he was. Possibly the Germans had been making inquiries in the district.

The boy did not come across the field, but from behind, having entered the wood at its southern end. Not knowing where Chalky would be hiding, he had surmised that he would be in some spot from which he could watch for the approach of Germans from the road. A smart boy, this boy. Now he was calling softly.

"M'sieu'? M'sieu' l'anglais? M'sieu' Eengleesh?"

"Here," Chalky called.

The lad's call had startled him, coming as it did from behind. The boy appeared through the trees, well-laden with what appeared to be a blanket roll.

"Ecoutez," he said, coming up to Chalky and kneeling down. He frowned, groping for the English words. "Listen. *Ne retournez pas à la route."* He made an impatient sound, tossed his head and gestured helplessly with his hands. *"Jairmans,"* he said, "beyond — beyond the cornair of the road, waiting. They 'ave see you, and they wait." He turned his head, spat into the bushes and made a defiant and very rude gesture in the direction of Yvetot.

"Le Boche!" he said with profound contempt. "Ver' stupid. *Très stupide. Nous allons les tricher."*
He saw incomprehension in Chalky's eyes and sighed theatrically. Then he smiled at him, gave him a conspiratorial wink, and opened the bundle. The two of them, the farmer from New Zealand and the farm boy of Normandy, bent over the revealed treasures like two seasoned plotters.

It was not, Chalky saw, a blanket, but an overcoat. Wrapped in it were foodstuffs — bread, cheese and hard-boiled eggs. There were cigarettes, and there were matches. The boy seemed to have thought of everything.

He proved to have been more thorough and far-seeing than Chalky had supposed, for now he brought forth from somewhere about his person a rather ink-stained French-English school dictionary and a railway timetable. While Chalky ate a couple of hard-boiled eggs and some cheese, the boy scrabbled through the dictionary, seeking the words he needed.

"There is a way for you to go," he said presently. "I show. I make... map."

He tore the fly-leaf from the railway timetable, produced a stub of pencil, licked it and quickly drew a sketch-map of Yvetot. When he had finished, he raised the pencil, sat back on his haunches and looked at it critically.

"Ça ira," he said, and spread it before Chalky. *"Voilà!"*

Chalky looked at it. The wood was represented by a triangular set of squiggles. An arrowed path led from it across a square which was obviously the dyked stubble field, to the roadway. The road took a right-angled turn to the left, and ran into an area of branching streets, plainly Yvetot. Some of the streets were named, and there was a building marked *"Gare,"* which sat beside a double line with cross-strokes like the rungs of a ladder. And, as if to make the meaning doubly clear, there was a crude representation of a railway engine with a smoking funnel.
"Parlez-vous français un peu, monsieur?" the boy asked.
To Chalky, the *"Parlez-vous français"* was recognisable.

"No," he said. *"Non.* Sorry."

"Then 'ow will you purchase un billet... a..." he riffled through the dictionary "... a ticket?" he finished.

But the question did not require an answer. The boy had all that worked out, too. He was a smart boy, a clever boy. He proceeded to rehearse Chalky in the business of buying a ticket for Paris — where to go, how to ask, what money to hand over, and, being a thrifty peasant, what change to expect.

"Ils pouvaient demander votre carte d'identité," he warned. At Chalky's blank look, he again thumbed through the dictionary.

"The *carte* — card of the identity. It is possible that they will demand to view," he explained.

"Ah, my identity card!" Chalky said. "She'll be right, son. I've got one."

The Flying Farmers of No. 485 Sqn.
From left: Sgt. G.A. Meagher (Brunnerton); Sgt. L.S.M. "Chalky" White, (Gore); W/O D.S. Macgregor, (Dunedin); Sgt. R.J. Stead, (Gisborne); Sgt. H.S. Tucker, (Palmerston North).

Members of 485 Sqn shortly before Chalky's escapade. Second from the left is P/O M.G. Sutherland, who was shot down and badly wounded in the same action as Chalky White, (extreme right).

With Chalky White, (2nd from left), are F/lt. R.W. Baker, later W/Cdr., (3rd from left), who commanded the squadron from March to June, 1943; W/Cdr. R.J.C. Grant, (4th from left), who commanded the squadron May 1942 to March 1943, and F/O Gibbs, (5th from left), who received Chalky's "Berlin" telephone call on his return.

"The Spitfire was the glamour aircraft of the war..." A group of 485 Sqn pilots with a Spitfire Mk. 9b, and their well-liked and highly respected champion, Sir William Jordan, New Zealand High Commissioner.

He showed the card which Monsieur Duhamel had obtained for him. The boy shook his head vehemently.

"Non, non, non, non!" he said. *"Elle n'a pas été . . ."* Again, the rapid dictionary search turned up the right words, more or less.

"Ah," said Chalky, nodding. "How do I get it stamped, then?"

The boy shook his head.

"Ce n'est pas possible. It is not possible," he said.

This amazing boy now opened his railway timetable.

"Vous voudriez aller au sud, à Paris, sans doute," he said, adding wisely, *"C'est à Paris que tous les anglais echappant se dirigent. C'est meilleur."* He looked at Chalky, sighed, and said, "All the English escapers go to Paris. It is best."

His fingers explored the columns of the timetable, and, after a moment, tired, perhaps, of struggling to express himself in English, he pointed to the appropriate details, saying, simply, *"Le train à Paris part d'Yvetot à trois heures et demie après midi."* Then, having received Chalky's nod of comprehension, he stood up.

"In Yvetot," he advised, "go to . . . to the . . . station." He made it sound like "stessyong," but Chalky had no difficulty in understanding him. "Go direct," the boy said. "Be wait in the stessyong."

"Thanks for the advice," Chalky said gratefully, "and thanks for — all this stuff — especially the coat. *Merci beaucoup,*" he finished.

"Ce n'est rien," the boy said off-handedly. He put out his hand, which Chalky engulfed in his own huge fist, and shook.

"Bonne chance, Anglais," he said, grinning, and turned and walked away, soon to be lost from sight amongst the trees and thickets.

Chalky looked at his watch. The time was almost a quarter to eleven. He decided to wait for another couple of hours before returning to the road. When he did, there was no one in sight, and he trudged towards the corner.

As he approached it, he began to feel a slight tingling of apprehension, which soon grew to a skin-crawling nervousness. He fought down a desire to creep up to the corner and peer around it, to see if the Germans had really gone. But he didn't, because furtiveness would label him unmistakably as a fugitive. Really, the only thing to do, the best thing to do, was to walk around that corner, stepping it out, whistling, as if he didn't have care in the world.

He marched up to the end of the embankment, turned the corner — and saw before him an empty road; and he had walked down it for a couple of yards before he realised that he was holding his breath. Soon afterwards, he entered the township of Yvetot.

Happily, the boy's sketch-plan was easy to follow. The street signs all turned up on cue, and Chalky arrived at the station at twenty minutes past three. With some misgivings, rehearsing himself like an actor in the phrases that the boy had given him, he approached the ticket window, hoping that the ticket clerk would not ask questions or try to engage him in conversation.

He stopped and peered through the window, and his eyes met the jaundiced stare of a man who obviously believed that afternoons were for peace and quiet, not to be disturbed by inconvenient customers with frivolous demands.

"Un billet de troisième classe à Paris, s'il vous plait, monsieur," Chalky requested, twisting tongue and tonsils around the unfamiliar vowel and consonant values. He thought he did rather well. At all events, the clerk thumbed a ticket from the dispenser and pushed it under the glass partition with one hand, simultaneously scooping in Chalky's money with the other. It seemed almost too easy to be true.

It was.

Chalky, surprised that there was, as yet, no train at the platform, looked at his watch, and then at the station clock. The clerk remarked, off-handedly, *"Le train est parti."*

Chalky looked at him blankly, then turned to walk away.

"Le train est parti!" the clerk said. He seemed to be getting excited about something. *"Je regrette, mais vous l'avez su, sans doute. Tout le monde le sait. L'indicateur est en temps français, notre temps. Pourquoi pas? C'est notre chemin de fer, et notre indicateur. Mais, hélas —"* he lifted eloquent shoulders and hands, and cocked his head on one side, *"le Boche ont le*

contrôle des chemins de fer, et ils se roulent par le temps allemand. Vous devez le savoir, n'est-ce pas? Vous ne pouviez pas l'ignorer." The hands and shoulders expressed again complete and tragic inability to do anything about — whatever he was talking about. Chalky, wondering what he was on about, continued to stare at him, trying to figure out just how to break off this one-sided conversation without arousing suspicion. In sudden exasperation, the clerk waved his hands excitedly and shouted: *"Le train est parti! Le train est parti!"*

Embarrassed, caught flat-footed by this unexpected and unwanted torrent of French, Chalky stood there. Something like dawning comprehension awoke in the clerk's face, unenlivened by anything suggesting friendliness. His mouth framed the word, *"Anglais,"* or so it seemed to Chalky, who wasted no time but retreated rapidly and got clear of the station as fast as he could. He walked rapidly through the streets of the town, not back towards Touffreville, but out towards Le Havre, until, beyond the outskirts of the town, he came upon a tumbledown shed on a roadside, not far from a cluster of farm buildings, and he ducked quickly into it.

Within was an old car, a Citroen, which he climbed into, subsiding on its broad back seat with a heartfelt sigh of relief. He had felt so very exposed, so very noticeable, out there on the road.

After a moment, he sat up and examined the car more closely. The cobwebs on the steering wheel and the thick dust on the seats confirmed his initial impression that it was, and had been for a considerable time, disused. He leaned back comfortably, then lit a cigarette. Really, he told himself, this was a vastly superior car to that in which he had spent the other night, when it rained. Better make, too. This was in the luxury class.

He finished his cigarette, then climbed out and explored the shed. There were some old petrol cans rusting in a corner, and two extremely threadbare Michelin tyres hanging on one wall. At the back of the shed was a window, thick with dust and cobwebs, and cracked right across, probably in the course of the shed's progressive leaning.

Chalky returned to the car and ate some of his store of food.

He smoked a second cigarette and wished that he had a bottle of beer. Then he began to wish that he had something to read. He remembered the timetable, and decided to check it, to find out when the next train for Paris would be leaving. Somehow, he understood, he had contrived to miss the last one. But he didn't, at that moment, feel up to struggling through a French timetable. He felt drained, and a lassitude was settling upon him. He got out of the car again and went to the window, from which he wiped some of the dust and cobwebs. And he stood, staring out at the fields.

There was a largish number of dairy cows, he observed, and he admired their condition, thinking about the thriftiness of the Norman peasant farmer. Each and every cow was tethered, and would presumably have to make do for the day on such grass as lay within the radius of the tether. There was no question of being a picky eater. When and only when she had grazed that circle about her stake thoroughly would she be moved to another, untouched spot. That was interesting. His own pasture management experience suggested that by the time the cow had eaten out the area around her stake, the ground would indeed have been grazed thoroughly; but because cows were not close grazers, the ground would still be in good heart, well manured and ready to come on again quickly. As for the cow, very little of the nourishment gained would have been burnt off in extensive wandering. That, he figured, was probably one of the reasons why the French peasant could wrest a reasonable living from an acreage which no New Zealand farmer would regard as an economic unit.

Chalky had plenty of time for such musing. He had, so his eventual perusal of the timetable suggested, all night to wait. The next train to Paris, as far as he could make out, would depart from Yvetot at ten-thirty next morning.

That was why he was fortunate in being a countryman. For a city man, the wait would have been a time of unrelieved, crushing boredom. Even Chalky found it irksome enough, but at least he could take an intelligent interest in his surroundings, in the evidence of husbandry that he saw about him.

But his mind kept returning to his experience at the Yvetot railway station. Half-past three, the timetable said. He was sure his watch was right — yet he had missed the afternoon's train. What's more, he had missed it by a considerable margin, or he would surely have heard its departure as he came through the town. Possibly the boy's timetable was out of date.

What Chalky did not know, what the ticket clerk had been trying to tell him, was that the French arranged train schedules and printed those times because it was their railway, and their timetable. If the Germans insisted on running trains to German time, the French railways people couldn't help that; and, presumably, if Germans missed trains through reading French timetables, it was just too bad, and they had only themselves to blame.

All Chalky knew, however, was that he was going to be at that railway station in good time to ensure that he didn't miss the ten-thirty tomorrow. He would be there an hour early, even if he had to shut himself in the station toilet to escape notice until the train pulled into the station.

In the meantime, he forced himself to be patient, succeeding to a remarkable degree in psyching himself into a sort of spurious contentment as he gazed from his window and watched the cows, reflecting on the farming practices he had seen, and examining them for any useful lessons they might contain. Doing so helped, somehow, to make Home a reality, and give some believability to the idea that he would get back to it alive and in one piece. His escape was thus more than a vague dream or a mere defiant gesture. It was a very real possibility — even a probability.

As dusk deepened, he ate some more of his food, wrapped himself in his newly acquired overcoat and, with regretful thoughts of the clean-sheeted, soft bed in Godefroi's cottage on the Duhamel estate, he presently drifted off to sleep.

He did not sleep well. In spite of the overcoat, the chill of the autumn night was too sharp to be ignored, and the back seat of a car too confined and too hard for real comfort. When dawn came at last, he greeted it thankfully, and, stiff and shivering, he crawled out of his bivvy. He ate some more of his food, standing to eat, stamping his feet, blowing on his chilled fingers. Autumn was not yet old enough for frosts, but outside, the fields were wet with heavy dew, and the dirty window was frosted with condensation.

Presently he got his few possessions together and stowed them in the canvas bag with his remaining food. He lit a cigarette and stuffed the packet into the pocket of his overcoat. Then, when he had finished his smoke, he let himself out of the shed and set out, back along the road to Yvetot.

He figured that he had plenty of time. As he walked into Yvetot, he heard a clock chime the quarter hour, he looked at his watch and found that it was still only a quarter past nine. So he sauntered through the streets. Yet, as he strolled across the road to the station, secure in the knowledge that it lacked an hour and two minutes to the scheduled time of his train, he was astounded to see that it already stood at the platform.

Indeed, the wheel-tapper, his hammer ringing faintly on the wheels, had already reached the last carriage. Chalky was pretty sure that in France, as in New Zealand, when the last wheel had been checked and passed inspection, the wheel-tapper would step up onto the platform, wave a negligent hand at the guard, and walk away. Then the guard would blow his whistle and wave his green flag, and the engine driver would release the brakes with a great hissing of compressed air, there would be a cacophony of clanking couplings, a hissing and whisping of steam, and the train would begin to move ponderously forward, gathering speed rapidly.

And it was happening!

Unless he put on a fast sprint, it would be gone, and he wouldn't be on it! He hurled himself forward, coat tails flying, boots flopping on his feet, clattering on the roadway. By the greatest of good fortune, there was no barrier control. He was able to dash forward without pause, dodging between groups of disembarked passengers, people seeing others off, and a porter with a rake of barrows. He reached a carriage, wrenched open the door and scrambled in, the shouts of a scandalised railway official in his ears.

The train was crowded. It was worse, Chalky thought, than a New Zealand Race Special. But he was not unused to Race Specials. He noticed that many of the double seats were occupied by three people; and, spying a minimal gap between two stolid peasants, he flopped into it, his hams working like the stern of an ecstatic terrier, boomps-a-daisying his way in.

Neither of his phlegmatic fellow occupants spared him more than the briefest of glances, and certainly neither showed the slightest inclination to engage him in conversation. He figured that they must have come from some other small community back along the thirty-odd miles of line between Yvetot and Le Havre, and that in their estimation, an inhabitant of Yvetot was practically a foreigner, unworthy of notice. Well, that suited him. He sat back as well as he was able, and began to feel secure and at peace with the world.

It was, therefore, a profound shock to the system to see a French ticket inspector enter the carriage at its far end, closely attended and carefully scrutinised by black-uniformed Gestapo....

6.

The entry of the Gestapo was blood-chilling. It was meant to be, of course. The uniform of sinister black, immaculately cut, with its dramatic red, white and black swastika armband, the skull-and-crossbones badge on the high-fronted cap, the shiny black boots, were meant to inspire awe. Even in civilian dress, the Gestapo leaned towards the dramatic — the belted leather raincoat and Fedora hat of the ruthless and cold-blooded gangster of the Hollywood movie. They were all, to a man, to a woman, bullies, sadists and, often, psychotics, the sweepings of the gutter veneered with a spurious air of cold, policemanlike impartiality. They were officered by bespectacled university types, coldly inhuman, wickedly intelligent.

Chalky, seeing them for the first time at close quarters, could not take them lightly. They filled him with an icy fear. But he was determined not to allow them to panic him. His anger rose again, sour in his mouth, hot on his neck, tingling in his muscles. He took refuge, as it were, behind a deliberate irreverence, telling himself that he didn't care for them, that he didn't want anything to do with such fancy-looking pricks; which was all very well — but how could he avoid them in the sardine-packed carriage of this crowded train?

For a man accustomed to New Zealand Race Specials, especially homeward bound Race Specials after a disastrous day, the question posed no insurmountable difficulty. He got up, slowly and casually, addressing mouthed but silent remarks to his neighbours. Then he sauntered easily towards the end of the compartment, lifting a hand in greeting to this passenger and that, clearly a regular on this line, known to one and all. The door of the compartment gave into a small foyer, much as in New Zealand carriages. In it stood a crush of passengers, all men. As Chalky opened the door, wider than was strictly necessary, most of them saw the Gestapo. Chalky closed the door behind him, unable any longer to keep up his pretence, and began to push and elbow his way towards the toilet. There was an element of resentful resistance. He produced his wings, and simultaneously someone near the door jerked a thumb at it and said, distinctly, "Gestapo." Immediately, comprehension replaced resentment on the faces of those he had been shoving, and a way was made for him. He ducked into the toilet, but did not shoot the bolt. He simply stood behind the door, which was very slightly ajar, holding it with one hand in case a sudden lurch of the train should swing it wide at an inconvenient moment. The bolt indicator, of course, proclaimed that the toilet was vacant.

As the ticket inspector opened the door from the compartment, two of the passengers began an argument with him, and by the time the Gestapo had managed to bully their way into the crush, everybody was arguing in vociferous French, with much violent gesticulation and appeals to heaven and the sacred name of Reason. Hands were reaching over other men's shoulders with tickets, the Gestapo were in danger of losing their elegant caps, the Inspector was arguing loudly, and all was confusion. As the Gestapo escaped into the next carriage with their dignity the Inspector raised his voice and, in his best official tone, read out the appropriate regulations from the back of the ticket. Suddenly it was all over.

Chalky waited for a few minutes more, then came out, to be greeted with grins and knowing winks. He did not return to his seat, but remained in the foyer, while his new friends kept an eye out against the return of the Gestapo. But they did not come back, and two hours later the train rolled into the Gare St Lazare, Paris.

With slight misgivings, Chalky left the train and followed the crowd, alert for any barrier control. There was none, and he simply walked out into the city, and the bright sunshine.

The day was hot, a dustier, more enervating heat than in the country. His overcoat began to attract the odd curious glance, and he decided to take it off and carry it over his shoulder. His battledress jacket was rolled up in his canvas bag, and in his blue issue pullover and shirtsleeves he felt slightly conspicuous; but he didn't think that it was a good idea to put on the battledress jacket, no matter how disguised it was, and anyway, nobody seemed to be taking any notice of him now.

The city was a fascinating place, with its cafés and shops, but its centre was too full of Huns to suit Chalky. It seemed that until he had had time to think out his next move, he had better keep out of the German's way. At escape lectures back at Biggin Hill, it had been suggested that the best place to find help was out in the suburbs, and certainly, as far as Chalky was concerned, any place where the Huns ran fewer to the acre was a sweeter and cleaner place, and one in which he was far less likely to be accosted by a Gestapo agent or some officious gendarme. Also, suburbs were places of gardened streets, of housewives and children, of peace and quiet and mind-your-own-business houses.

So he wandered with slightly more purpose, looking for a bus stop. More or less by accident, he found an ornate entrance to the Métro, the French equivalent of London's Tube. (It wasn't hard to find. Nowhere in the French capital is more than 500m from the admirable Métro. Neither was there much difficulty in buying a ticket, since on the Métro there is no need to ask for a specific destination or number of sections. A booklet of tickets may be obtained for a few francs, and these are valid for any journey on any line, no matter how long or short.)

At first it was rather pleasant, out in the suburbs, which were drowsy and still in the warm autumn sunshine. The only trouble was, the houses and gardens were hidden behind high walls and locked gates, and he saw nobody on the streets at all. He had no idea of where he was, but he made a careful mental note of each corner he turned, and each street he travelled along, in order that he might find his way back to the Métro terminus.

In the event, he did not return to it. He began to realise that wandering about the surburban streets of a great city was even more lonely than wandering in open country. In the country you were, to some degree, part of the scenery. The emptiness of the fields was expected and right, and, since you were part of the scene, not really emptiness. Here, however, you were conscious of being in the midst of vast numbers of people, of families in family homes — yet they seemed to belong to another realm, a different reality of which you were not a part. For all they knew of you, for all of the impact you had on their existence, for all they seemed to care, you might have been a ghost, unseen, unsuspected, unreal. Chalky felt, with slight bitterness, that this was something that didn't seem to have occurred to those who lectured on escape techniques. It was all very well to suspect that the suburbs were places where you should go for help; but how in hell could you get help from street after street of locked gates?

The Métro tickets, as far as he could tell from the odd recognisable word on the cover of the ticket booklet, were also valid for buses, so when one pulled into a curbside stop nearby, he boarded it and proffered his ticket booklet. The conductor took a ticket without comment, and Chalky sat back and allowed the bus to carry him wheresoever it would. With no idea of where he was, or to where he might be heading, he sat and looked out at the passing streets, and enjoyed being off his painful feet again.

The bus meandered through street after street of locked gates and closed doors until it came to the end of its run and, like any other bus, turned about and made its way back to the city centre, with its gendarmes and Germans and the hunted feeling it gave him. So he resorted to the Métro again near the Hotel de Ville, and rode it through the suburban stations of Rambuteau and Goncourt, at each of which hundreds of home-going, six o'clock Frenchmen disembarked. It reminded him of the Hutt Valley commuter trains out of Wellington, except that this one was underground, in an eternal tunnel.

There seemed to be no Germans on the train, but the crowds made it difficult to see who might be approaching through the carriages, and he was afraid of being caught in a Gestapo check. He was profoundly glad, therefore, when many of the passengers left at the interchange station of Belleville. The train, now somewhat relieved of the six o'clock crush, slid onwards, depositing passengers at the suburban stations of Pyrénées and Jourdain. By the time it arrived at the interchange station of Place des Fêtes, it was almost empty, and here Chalky decided to leave it also. He wasn't sure what to do next, but he could hardly sit on the train all night. For the first and only time in his life, he envied the home-going city workers, the pale commuters between office and suburban house. He began to wonder just where he would spend the night.

At Les Lilas, in a surburban shopping centre, he found a cafe, a dark little den of a place below street level. He went down worn stone steps, opened the door and peered into the gloomy interior. There were only two customers in the place, both men, neither of whom spared him a glance. If nothing else, Chalky told himself, it would be a good spot for a quick meal. It was dark, and a man sitting at a table in such a place sipping coffee would be inconspicuous. But he would be even less noticeable to any passing gendarme or — perish the thought! — Gestapo snoop if he were to join the other two customers. So he entered, and sat himself down with the two Frenchmen.

If you walk into a New Zealand coffee bar and casually seat yourself at an already occupied table, you will almost certainly, by words or looks or indignant body language, be made to feel somewhat superfluous. In a French café you receive, at most, a disinterested glance, and your right to the vacant chair, and to your privacy, goes unchallenged — which, Chalky acknowledged, was no doubt very civilised, and all right as far as it went. But he wanted to look as if he belonged in the company of these two men, a regular, perhaps, in the cafe, one of the natives. So he nudged one of them, and when they both looked at him interrogatively and little indignantly, he groped in his pants pocket and brought out his closed fist, which he opened on the table top to disclose his RAF wings.

There was a sharp intake of breath, the two Frenchmen looked at each other, and again at Chalky. Then one of them turned in his chair and made urgent hand signals of a theatrically conspiratorial nature towards the dark, far corner where the espresso coffee machine grumbled on the end of the counter. The shadows behind the machine stirred and resolved themselves into the slightly stout figure of *Madame la Propriétaire,* who now advanced upon the table. The Frenchman who had beckoned to her looked again at Chalky, and then at his friend.

"C'est son affaire," he said, shrugging. *"Elle peut s'en occuper."* It is her affair. Let her see to it. Chalky understood perfectly. It was implicit in the man's tone, and in the way in which he rose from his chair, indicated Chalky to Madame with a "He's all yours" gesture, and left the premises with his friend.

Madame came and stood beside Chalky, arms akimbo, a sturdy grandmother with whom it was clearly unwise to muck about. She cocked her head and, by her posture and the expression on her face, plainly invited Chalky to give an account of himself. After a moment's hesitation, Chalky opened his fist again and displayed his wings. Madame showed neither alarm nor hostility, which encouraged him to stay put when she commanded, *"Attendez!"*

She disappeared into some nether region, and Chalky began a fierce debate with himself as to whether he should wait or run. He had not exactly been welcomed with open arms. On the contrary, the attitude of the two customers seemed to suggest that they desired no part of him. And Madame had given him not one word of welcome or encouragement, but had gone rushing off to fetch someone else — perhaps a gendarme?

On the other hand, she had not seemed over-perturbed by his presence in her cafe, and if he was to go rushing off whenever people asked him to wait, he would never receive any help at all. You had to trust someone, sooner or later. So he sat and waited.

After about five minutes the strain became intolerable, and he was on the point of rising to slip quietly away, to make his way back to the Métro and find himself another surburb. But just as he pushed back his chair, Madame reappeared. With her was a smartly uniformed gendarme.

Chalky's immediate impulse was to run. But it occurred to him that these people were, after all, French — allies. And so far neither had done anything to alarm him. They might, gendarme or no gendarme, be disposed and able to help him. If not — well, he figured that he should be able to handle an old woman and a slightly-built, youngish policeman.

"Are you English?" the gendarme asked. His accent was definitely Maurice Chevalier.

"Yes," Chalky replied warily. "RAF." He showed his wings, and this time, his New Zealand flashes.

"Ah," the gendarme said. He turned to Madame, and his smile was as Maurice Chevalier as his accent. *"Nouvelle Zélande!"* he enthused. *"L'aviateur est —"*

"Nouvelle Zélande," Madame agreed, nodding and smiling. *"Si loin de chez vous,"* she added, assuming an expression of utter tragedy.

"So far from 'ome," the gendarme translated. "If it pleases you," he said, with a sudden switch to a brisk and businesslike manner, "come with me."

Chalky looked from one to the other.

"Where to?" he asked.

"You will be safe," the gendarme assured him.

Chalky hesitated for a moment longer, then picked up his coat and his canvas bag.

"Merci beaucoup, Madame," he said to the old lady.

"Ce n'est rien," she assured him.

Still wary, though pretending to relax, Chalky followed the gendarme. It was reassuring, somehow, that they went out the back way, picking their way through a narrow passageway, past a litter of rubbish cans, wooden crates, mops and brooms — and that the policeman led the way. If it had been his intention to arrest him, Chalky felt, he would have been marched through the front door and up into the main shopping thoroughfare as a trophy of the chase, a triumph, a testimony to the gendarme's skill and bravery and a warning of the power of the Law. Going out the back way seemed to suggest that the gendarme didn't want any publicity, and the fact that he led the way meant that Chalky could get away if he chose. Even so, Chalky was aware, from his escape lectures, that there was a reward of ten thousand francs offered for the capture of an allied airman — a big inducement, especially to an underpaid gendarme who probably had a wife and family to keep, and who possibly had to rely on the black market for some of their basic needs. So he remained on the alert, watching the street ahead for any indication of the presence of a police station. It was, therefore, with considerable relief that he was led into one of a row of small suburban houses, to be met in its hallway by the gendarme's attractive young wife.

The gendarme stepped forward and kissed her, then turned to Chalky.

"Ma chérie, je te présente l'aviateur anglais — l'aviateur neo-zélandais," he corrected.

"RAF?" she asked.

"Yes," Chalky told her. "Pleased to meet you. My name is White, Leslie White. But my friends call me Chalky."

"Pardonnez-moi," she apologized. "I do not speak English, only a little."

In the pleasant living room, she introduced him to her two small children simply as *"l'ami de Papa."* Children of that age could be expected to mention such a visit at inconvenient moments. If they referred to the visitor merely as "Papa's friend," no great harm would be done.

They fed Chalky a good, substantial meal, after which the gendarme produced a timetable for trains to the Vichy frontier. Together, he and Chalky selected a train, and Chalky was intrigued to notice that this timetable had been pencil-amended. He mentioned the trouble he had had catching a train from Yvetot, and the gendarme explained to him about the difference between German and French times. The amendments in the gendarme's timetable conformed to the German schedules.

He ascertained that Chalky had enough money, wrote down the name of the town to which he should travel, then bade him a friendly farewell. It was all done so matter-of-factly, so efficiently, that Chalky suspected that he was not the first escaper to be assisted by this amiably efficient gendarme.

The policeman's wife now took Chalky out into the street. They walked for some distance, through streets and boulevards and alleys, until at length they came to an hotel, where she introduced him to the proprietress, a stately, handsome dame, slightly formidable, who nevertheless greeted him with grave kindliness. The gendarme's wife took her leave, explaining in a mixture of French and English that she had less than an hour to curfew, and wished to be home, off the streets.

Madame called an attractive young woman from a lounge opening off the foyer, and instructed her in rapid French. The young woman led Chalky up flights of stairs and along passages with firmly closed doors. They walked beneath ornate architraves with looped-back velvet curtains, and up yet another flight of stairs. Presently she brought him to a room, and ushered him in. So far, she had not spoken. She stood there, in the room, smiling at him, delighted at the pleasure which chased across his face when he saw that the bed was large and soft, and flung himself down upon it gladly with a long-drawn "A-a-a-h!" of satisfaction. Then his guide gave him a mock-rueful look, and laughingly left him with a warm and slightly husky "Good night, RAF."

It was not precisely a quiet hotel, for all that it was out in the suburbs. In spite of his weariness, he was kept awake for some time, and once or twice awakened out of sleep, when at last he had dropped off, by comings and goings, giggling and murmuring in the corridor. But at last exhaustion had its way, and he sank into a deep slumber.

He was awakened by Madame herself, with a cup of coffee.

"It is time for you to depart," she said in her oddly formal English. "When you are prepared, come downstairs for *un petit déjeuner*; and per'aps we can supply some food for your journey."

In the dining room, Chalky was surprised to find that all the other guests were women, all of them young, all attractive, each with a certain indefinable *chic*, who eyed him and whispered and giggled as he sat at a small table with Madame, eating croissants and sipping coffee. Two or three of them crossed the room to be introduced, and it became apparent that they were carrying information back to the others.

"Where will you go?" Madame wondered.

"I thought I'd catch a train to the South of France," Chalky confided. She gave him an impression of trustworthiness.

"It would be best," she agreed.

"Gare Austerlitz," Chalky said.

Madame told him where to find the Métro, and which train to take.

"Thank you," Chalky said.

"I must tell you," Madame said, "that there is a frontier between Vichy France and Occupied France."

"I know," Chalky said. "The demarcation line is marked on my map."

"It is something more than a demarcation line," Madame warned. "There are border checks."

"Border posts? Armed guards and that sort of thing?"

"Not to my knowledge," Madame replied, "but there is close German and Vichy police surveillance, train checks and other impudences. Through the middle of France!" she said indignantly. "It is not to be borne!" Practically, she added, "It is possible to proceed via Bourges or Tours."

"I was told to go by way of Bourges," Chalky told her. She winced at his accent, but nodded.

"That is wisest. Bourges — *Bourges* —" she said the name twice, the second time with slow emphasis, correcting his pronunciation "is hardly a city. A provincial town. At Tours there are... difficulties. At Bourges, the Boche are certain to be watchful, but the town is less important. It would be wise to leave the train at Bourges and cross the demarcation line on foot. Catch another train when you are far to the south of it; per'aps at Issoudun."

"How far is Issoudun from the Vichy frontier?" Chalky asked, thinking of his ingrown toenails.

"About thirty kilometres. Per'aps forty."

"Thanks," Chalky said. "If I take the train to Bourges —" Madame winced again at his accent.

"Write it down," she directed.

"I've got it written down," Chalky assured her.

"Then show it to the ticket seller. Do not speak it." She sighed and shook her head.

The girls crowded into the lobby to see him off, offering fragments of advice, touching him, smiling.

"Prenez garde! Faites attention!" (Take care of yourself.)

"Revenez, RAF!" (Come back, RAF.)

"Restez ici, avec nous, RAF," invited one, going one better.

"Prenez garde du Boche, RAF," (Avoid the Boche, RAF), another said, and they all looked grave.

Chalky walked out in a soft, perfumed cloud of goodwill. It was, he thought, a nice hotel. Nice, friendly people. Odd, that all the guests were girls. As he walked to the Métro, it suddenly dawned on him why all the guests were girls. And if, to a new, less innocent generation such slowness seems naive, or even improbable, it should be remembered that Chalky, while not unfamiliar with the concept, with the fact, had never in all his life, until now, been in a brothel. If they existed in New Zealand, they certainly did not dwell flamboyantly in ornate and public hotels. Not in Gore, anyway, and not in Invercargill.

He took the Métro to the Gare Austerlitz, which, when he found it, was just about the biggest railway station he had ever seen. He wandered about the place, looking for some sign that would identify the platform from which the train to Bourges would leave. His obvious bewilderment attracted the attention of a French railway official, who promptly came over to him.

"Qu'est-ce que vous cherchez, monsieur?" he asked.

Chalky looked at him blankly.

"Vous allez quelque part? Où vous attendez a quelqu'un peut-être?" the man wanted to know.

Chalky looked about him. It crossed his mind that he might have to clobber this character and make a dash for it.

The official's manner did not change. Looking at Chalky steadily, he demanded: *"Votre carte d'identité, s'il vous plait, monsieur."*

There was no question of running away, Chalky saw. Out of the tail of his eye he saw uniformed Germans strolling about the concourse. *"Carte d'identité"* was a recognisable phrase. He thought he had better produce it. Unstamped, it might still fool this official, whoever he was. It had been given to Chalky to use as a last resort, and he couldn't imagine a laster resort than this one. He dug into his pocket and brought forth the card.

The official examined it for a long moment, then looked at Chalky, who met his stare with difficulty, but managed a guileless stare in spite of his inner turmoil. The man grinned and gave him back his card, and pointed to the exit. Chalky returned his grin nervously, walked to the indicated exit, and found himself in a foyer with ticket windows along one side. He picked one at random, walked up to it and spread his slip of paper and his money on the counter. The female ticket clerk looked at it. Then she eyed Chalky shrewdly, took a ticket from the dispenser and counted money from the cash he had laid before her, pushing the ticket and the remainder of the money back to him. She winked and whispered: "Good luck, *Anglais*."

Greatly heartened, Chalky asked, "Where is the train?"

She pointed, and off he went.

There was one more hurdle. At the barrier an official stood. He wore ordinary civilian clothes, and there was no way of knowing whether he was an official of the French railways or a policeman, or possibly even a Gestapo agent. Chalky thought that he looked like a Frenchman, and reaching him, looked at him with frank blue eyes, and trustfully spoke one of his few French words.

"Anglais," he said.

The man looked at him expressionlessly, checked his ticket and waved him through without a word.

The train was not over-full, and Chalky had no trouble obtaining a seat. As he settled down in it, the official who had examined his identity card strolled past. He looked in, saw Chalky and grinned again. Then the train started, huffing and clanking and jerking, and pulled away from the platform, out through the station, rattling over the points in the marshalling yards, gathering speed. It fled through still, closed surburbs, past the sidings of the electrical machinery factories at Ivry, and the chemical and glassware works around Vitry. It curved around the boundary of Orly Airport, (where Chalky was professionally interested to observe Junkers transports with their slab-sided, corrugated, swastika-banded fuselages and drag-ringed radial engines, as well as some JU88s.) And then the train was clear of, free from, Paris.

Chalky settled back comfortably. A man came through the carriage selling newspapers and magazines; Chalky purchased a paper and a couple of illustrated journals, figuring that if he couldn't read them, at least he could look at the pictures. He opened the paper and pretended to read. He would rather have sat and gazed out the window at the passing countryside, but reading was a good protection against any attempt by the man sitting next to him to engage him in conversation.

But it was a difficult exercise. Chalky's loneliness was against it. It was the very loneliness of this adventure that tended to grind him down. Therefore, when he found in the newspaper a map of the Pacific theatre, he could not resist nudging his neighbour, pointing at New Zealand on the map, producing his wings and New Zealand flashes and saying, as he pointed to himself, "Me! *Nouvelle Zélande.*"

The startled passenger looked at him in alarm, and hastily changed his seat. Disappointed, Chalky sighed and told himself that he might well have reacted in the same way. After all, the man was just an ordinary, respectable citizen, going quietly about his business, not wanting to be involved in confrontations with the French police or the railway officials, and most assuredly not with the Gestapo! Chalky, fortified by the encouragement he had received at the railway station, smiled indulgently. The man had obviously led a quiet life, and wasn't used to danger, as Chalky was. When you've had a few narrow squeaks, you aren't so easily scared, he thought.

And then the ticket inspector entered the carriage, and he was quickly aware that no matter now many narrow squeaks you had had, you never really got used to it, and that he himself was as reluctant as his erstwhile seat-mate to face up to probing, blustering officialdom. After all, his experience so far suggested that when a French ticket inspector arrived, the Gestapo were likely to be close behind. He therefore vacated his seat and tried the old loo trick again.

This time, it didn't work. The inspector stood outside the toilet, patiently but insistently knocking; and Chalky, mindful of the fact that it was as well to face the inspector, if possible, before the Gestapo arrived, came out. After all, he did have a ticket.

The inspector examined Chalky's ticket, punched it and handed it back. There were no Germans after all, fortunately; for the man stood there, offering reiterated apologies. He was sorry that he had had to disturb *M'sieu'*, but what would you? He hoped that *m'sieur'* had not been discommoded — so to speak — and implored him not to be embarrassed, and to please return to the toilet if he felt so inclined. It was all delivered in rapid-fire French, with shrugs, pursings of the lips, expressive eyebrows, tiltings of the head and graphic hand gestures which left Chalky in very little doubt as to what was being said. He patted the inspector forgivingly on the shoulder, smiled at him and returned to his seat.

At Bourges, a town of some 60,000 people, Chalky left the train, to be faced immediately with the problem of where to go for help. He really knew nothing about the demarkation line between Occupied France and Vichy France, except that it lay about eight kilometres south of Bourges, and ran with the River Cher between Bourges and Tours. But he believed that it was bound to be patrolled. He decided to cross it somewhere south of Bourges, which was too full of Huns for comfort, and he determined to go south by train. He found, from signs on the platform, that trains ran from Bourges to three destinations — Paris, Tours and Moulins. A furtive examination of his map told him that Moulins was south-east of Bourges, and that the railway plunged southward from there into Vichy France.

However, there were no trains in at the moment, and he had no idea of how long he might have to wait. With the number of Germans milling about the place, he began to get nervous, and decided to get out into the suburbs. From just outside the station, he took a tram, which headed east, almost to the gates of a large German camp, soldiery from which crowded into the tram. Unhappily Chalky stayed in his seat, trying to be as inconspicuous as possible, hoping against hope that none of the soldiers would speak to him. The tram ground its bone-jarring way back into town on a loop line; and when it pulled up near the railway station, Chalky left it, walking away from the station in the midst of a crowd of laughing soldiers obviously bent on a night on the town.

He parted company with them without regret and, conscious of the fact that he had to find somewhere to spend the night before the curfew began, made his way westward, heading for the village of Marmagne, which was closer than Bourges to the Vichy border, and from which, so his map told him, a railway line branched southward.

It was, as always, a nerve-racking business, walking through the town. Particularly at its centre, you had the feeling that you were conspicuous, that all eyes were upon you, that at any moment some French gendarme or a Gestapo agent might accost you and demand to see your papers. Chalky tried to walk at a normal pace, but found himself almost running from time to time, whereupon he would slow to a dawdle. No one questioned his progress, and as the business centre fell behind him, Chalky began to feel easier.

Near the edge of town, and from time to time as he passed by the diminishing straggle of houses beyond the outskirts, he approached small groups of people, middle-class citizens in business suits, and their patently suburban wives. On each occasion they were friendly enough when he explained, as best he could, who he was and what he was, and displayed his RAF wings. But as soon as he began to ask for help, they cooled off noticeably.

Typically, Chalky did not blame them. He knew well enough the danger they faced, and he was aware of the efforts made by the Gestapo to entrap them into the "crime" of aiding and abetting Allied escapers. He saw, too, their anxious, careworn faces, and the threadbare clothes — the business suits shiny with much brushing, the frocks enlivened with small, contrived touches of decoration in a brave effort to disguise their worn-out shapelessness and to achieve a little chic; and so he smiled at them, sympathising, and thanked them anyway, and moved on, disliking the Hun even more.

He arrived at Marmagne at dusk, and experienced again the daunting business of choosing a house at which to ask for help. There was, of course, no real basis for assessment. It was really just a straw-drawing process, as rational as his method of deciding which of the two compasses to keep, and every bit as liable to be every bit as wrong.

He would readily have walked up to the first house from whose door a ray of light shone out into the deepening dusk, on the vague notion that an open door would surely betoken trustfulness and hospitality. But there was only one open door, one ray of light, and that was from a small *estaminet,* which he entered, and ordered beer. That was easy enough. The French and the English words sounded near enough the same, and your average peasant ordered his beer in a gruff monosyllable, without a please or a thankyou.

The proprietor did not radiate friendliness, as it happened He was not actively hostile, but merely surly. Maybe, Chalky thought, he's had a bad day, and is anxious to shut up shop. So he swallowed his beer and walked out into the street, where he promptly collided with a teenage boy.

"Sorry," he said without thinking.

"It is nothing," the boy said. Then he stared at Chalky. Another, slightly older boy, and a teenage girl, also stared at him.

"Anglais!" the older boy breathed.

"You speak English?" Chalky asked.

"I speak English, very good," the first boy promised. "But not here. Come to our house."

They seized his arms and propelled him along the street, across the road and up the steps of a house. He pulled back slightly at the top of the steps, and looked both ways, up and down the street.

"It is all right," the boy said.

Maybe it was. But there was a stillness, a darkness about the street and about this house that momentarily sapped his confidence. There were no doors open, no rays of light. Even the *estaminet* lights had gone out. Under the monstrous, all-covering Nazi bureaucracy, even in Marmagne, an inconsiderable village in the very heart of France, far from fortifications and defences, possessing no vital factories, occupied by no important headquarters, to fail to maintain a complete blackout was not merely to risk a fine, but to court a cruel imprisonment or execution.

There was a long and pregnant pause, when the whole village seemed to be watching and listening from behind darkened windows. And then the door opened, the merest fraction. He would never have noticed that it had opened, had it not squeaked slightly on its hinges.

"Que voulez-vous?" a woman's voice asked. She sounded sharp and unfriendly.

"I need help," Chalky said.

"Allez-y," the woman said, and made to close the door. Chalky, knowing that there was no point in trying to force his attentions on anyone, began to turn away. But suddenly the girl pushed the door open, and the woman was revealed, silhouetted against the dim light from some back room, visible enough for Chalky to see that she was surveying him from his head to his toes and back to his head again.

"Qui est-ce que?" she asked the youngsters.

The elder boy opened his mouth to explain, but realised that he didn't know the answer.

"Qui est-ce que vous êtes, monsieur?" he asked.

Chalky, reading the boy's meaning from his inflection and expression, replied: *"Anglais,* RAF." He produced his wings and flashes. *"Nouvelle Zélande,* actually," he said.

"Dites-lui de s'en aller," the woman commanded the children, not very hopefully. *"Entrez et fermez la porte — tout de suite!"*

They took not the slightest notice, but gathered around Chalky more closely, fingering his wings and eagle badges, holding them up to what faint light there was.

"Nouvelle Zélande," the girl said thoughtfully.

"RAF," the younger boy breathed in the tone in which a Saxon lad might have whispered "Robin Hood!"

"Eteins la lumière, Maman," the girl suggested, and Maman gladly went down the hall and closed the door on the offending light, then came back and stood, shadowy and indistinct yet plainly distracted with fear, in the doorway. Chalky understood and sympathised.

"Perhaps I'd better go," he said to the youngsters. But these kids were teenagers, and by the almost breathless excitement in their voices, this was plainly the very essence of High Adventure.

"Nous allons vous aider," one of the boys said.

"We will 'elp," the other boy translated.

"Il doit avoir une cachette," the girl said practically. *"Maman, l'aviateur anglais, il doit avoir une cachette."*

"My sister is say to Maman that we must 'ide you," the English-speaking boy told Chalky. Maman raised her hands towards heaven, muttering. Then she shrugged.

"Mon Dieu! Est-ce que vous allez informer tout le monde? Vous voulez que tout la population de Marmagne s'en sait? Entrez, vite!"

"Maman is afraid the entire town will 'ear us," the boy told Chalky, laughing. "Come into the 'ouse."

Chalky found himself impelled by eager hands, past Maman, into the dark hall. The door was closed behind them, the light switched on again. Maman stood looking at them crossly.

"Eh bien? Qu'est-ce que vous avez fait?" she asked her children.

"Ça ira, Maman!" the English-speaking boy assured her. "It will be all right," he said in English, for Chalky's benefit.

Maman humphed and looked at Chalky.

"Pourquoi vous êtes arrivé chez moi?" she demanded. Again, her tone and the fear in her eyes made her meaning abundantly clear. She wanted to know why, of all the houses in Marmagne, he had to come to her house.

"I don't want to cause you any trouble," Chalky said.

The youngsters, meanwhile, had withdrawn a little way down the hall, and were having a conference. Chalky assumed that it was serious, though he was intrigued by the fact that it was punctuated by the odd giggle. He and Maman stood facing one another, both looking worried, Maman for fear that Chalky's advent would bring the wrath of the Germans down upon her head, Chalky by the uncomfortable feeling that these kids might, by taking matters too lightly, lead themselves and him into trouble. And both Chalky and Maman were frustrated by the maddening communciations barrier.

But at last the elder of the two boys came to her.

"Nous allons l'emmener à la ferme," he said.

"We are take you to a farm," the younger boy translated.

"Il aura un couvert assuré — et ils connaissent ce qu'il faut faire lui aider."

It is safe," the younger boy told Chalky, "and they . . . they . . . know 'ow to 'elp."

Maman nodded, still looking worriedly at Chalky.

"Oui, ça serait pour le mieux." She nodded more positively. *"Oui. Oui. Faites comme bon vous semble. Mais faites attention!"* She was giving them reluctant permission to do as they thought best, with a warning to them to be careful.

"Oui, Maman, ça ira. Ne t'inquiète pas," the girl said.

"Maman is worry," the younger boy explained to Chalky unnecessarily. "My sister inform her will be OK."

They hustled Chalky out to the back of the house, where Maman switched off the light and opened the back door. Chalky, in the darkness, touched her arm and seized and shook her hand in his immense fist, and said, *"Merci beaucoup, Madame."*

She still did not answer him, but once more admonished the children.

"Faites attention! J'ai peur. C'est trop dangereux!" (Have a care. I am afraid. It is too dangerous.)

"Oui, Maman," the girl said, in that impatient, slightly patronising tone that teenagers the world over use to fussing parents. Then Maman shut the door firmly, and the youngsters led Chalky across the enclosed kitchen garden, through a small door in a high back fence, and out into one of those blank-walled alleys which slip between the backyards of homes in many European towns.

They tried to be cautious, but this, after all, was an Adventure, and their high spirits bubbled up again and again, in snatches of excited chatter, ripples of laughter, and much mutual shushing. Chalky could not help smiling in their merry company. He strode along, towering above them, a battle cruiser amid a screen of destroyers, a heavy bomber escorted by nimble, slim fighters. The girl grasped his arm, and one of the brothers touched the other from time to time, almost as if he suspected that Chalky was a dream figure who might disappear at any moment without warning.

They were more subdued, however, as they emerged from the lane into a wider street. There were no people about, but it was always possible that a German motor patrol might sweep around a corner, even in a backwater like Marmagne, ready to arrest anyone found on the streets.

Just outside the village, they left the road and walked across a couple of fields. Chalky did not know it at the time, but the Vichy demarkation line was less than a kilometre away. In the darkness of the somewhat cloudy night, they came presently to a stable, and here the youngsters prepared to leave Chalky, after taking him to a row of stalls, in each of which was a working bullock and manger filled with sweet-smelling hay. One boy and the girl slipped away immediately. Chalky saw them briefly in the lighter square of the open doorway. The other boy, not whispering but keeping his voice pitched conspiratorially low, gave Chalky final instructions.

"I go now," he said. *"M'sieu' RAF,* wait 'ere. If a... une personne... should come, 'ide in the straw. If it is that it is a friend, there will be knocking — so — on the door. If no knocking, remain 'ide. We will come back soon, with 'ot food from the... the 'ouse of the farm. They are friends, the people."

He too, left the stable, and Chalky chose a stall and slipped into it, patting its patient occupant on the rump, ruffling the top of its polled head, and hoisting himself up, to sit on the edge of its manger.

"Don't mind me, sport," he said. The ox blew hay-scented breath in his face, and Chalky talked to it quietly, stroking its nose, rubbing its neck. Then he tumbled back into the manger and pulled straw over himself.

"Try not to hog all the bedclothes," he told the ox.

He lay there for almost half an hour before he heard footsteps outside the stable, and the knock on the door. As he climbed from the manger and brushed the hay from his person, a match flared, and Chalky saw dark figures, indistinct about a hurricane lamp, in a growing nimbus of light. He heard the creak and clap of the lamp glass being lowered, and then the lamp was held up, revealing the pale faces of the children.

"Come out, *M'sieu' RAF,*" the English-speaking boy invited. "We 'ave bring food."

As Chalky came forth from his stall, still brushing himself down, the girl spread a napkin on an upturned box and placed upon it a knife, a fork and a covered plate.

"Venez, maintenant," the older boy said urgently. He was standing near the stable door.

"Au revoir, et bonne chance," the girl said. Chalky took her small, slim hand.

"We 'ave to go," the younger boy told Chalky, and put out his hand. Chalky solemnly shook both boys' hands.

"Say thank you to your mother for me," he requested, "and tell her I'm sorry I worried her. And thanks very much, all of you. I'll never forget."

They melted away across the fields, and Chalky went back into the stable, shutting the door and turning up the lamp. The plate, he found, held a heaped portion of some kind of ragout with vegetables. The meat he identified as rabbit. On the floor by the box he discovered a bottle of wine and an ordinary kitchen tumbler. He drank the first glass to quench his thirst, and then had another glass for pleasure. But in his drinking he was sparing — for Chalky — because he wanted to have his wits about him, wanted to sleep reasonably lightly, and not be caught in a half-drunken slumber. Ordinarily, one bottle of red *vin ordinaire* wouldn't have fazed him, for he had a hard head; but he was tired to the point of exhaustion in spite of last night's comfortable bed, and he had not eaten very much until now, and — well, it was better to play it safe.

Yet he did sleep soundly, not to say heavily, with the ox breathing on him and the hay covering him warmly, and it was broad daylight when he was awakened by the rattle of the opening door. If there had been a knock, he must have slept through it. He was wide awake, now, but remained concealed in the hay.

"Come out, RAF," a man's voice said in English. It was impossible to tell whether it was an invitation or a command.

Peering out from the manger, Chalky saw a man in civilian clothes. He supposed that this must be the farmer, though he looked, somehow, unfarmerlike. The light in this stable was not the best, and the man was, in any case, silhouetted against the open doorway, and the details of his appearance were not readily discernible. It was just that.... But Chalky couldn't be sure what it was. One thing was certain. Whoever he was, he knew Chalky was there.

It was not until he had clambered from the manger and squeezed past the ox to the open end of the stall that Chalky realised why the man had not looked like a farmer. He was dressed in a business suit, with a collar and tie.

7.

It isn't easy to define "farmer" in terms of general appearance. All Chalky knew was that none of the farmers of his acquaintance got around the place in lounge suits and ties. Office workers did, and civil servants did, and doctors, and lawyers, and plain-clothes policemen, and — Gestapo?

He paused for a moment before stepping out of the stall, as this thought struck him. Then he shrugged it off — metaphorically, because he was not a man to signal his punches — and stooped as though to tie a shoe lace, then stood again and stepped confidently forth. Before him he saw a man of medium height, grave-faced, yet with a friendly enough look in his eyes.

"Did you sleep well?" he asked pleasantly. His accent was slight, giving his English a lilt that Chalky found engaging.

"Yes, thanks," he said. He was still a little uncertain. But he had begun, with eyes trained by experience, to notice things about the man which were somehow reassuring. It was difficult to estimate his age, for example. His face was a little careworn, the face of a man who has been too long under tension. The suit was neat and well-pressed, but — not quite threadbare, but well worn. A Gestapo man would have a better suit than that.

"This," the man said, waving a hand about the interior of the stable, "is my place. I'm sorry I did not come to you earlier, but I thought it best to stay clear until the workmen were well away."

Chalky relaxed. His day, he felt, had started well. Not only was he being hidden and fed by a friendly Frenchman, but also, the man spoke English.

Chalky began to speak, realising he was probably saying more than he should, but quite unable to stop himself, so great was his longing for conversation.

"Pleased to meet you," he said. "My name's White, Leslie White. Everyone calls me Chalky. You just don't know how good it is to be able to speak English with someone!" He fished his wings and his New Zealand tabs out of his pocket and displayed them, somewhat soiled, in his not over-clean hand. "RAF," he finished unnecessarily.

"Yes," the man said.

"I'm — grateful to you for letting me use your stable," Chalky told him.

"It is nothing."

"It's a bloody lot to me," Chalky said feelingly. "I — the children, last night. Will I see them again?"

"No," the man said positively. He added, "What children?"

"The children who —" Chalky began, then stopped and grinned. "Oh. Oh, well, it's just that I wanted to thank them."

"It is better you have no further contact. There were no children."

"No, I suppose not," Chalky agreed.

"There were no children," the man repeated positively. He moved towards the door, but turned again.

"Come with me," he directed. Seeing Chalky hesitate, he smiled. "To the house. You need food, and you would no doubt be glad of a bath. And then we shall see what is to be done about you."

Chalky was not at all keen on the phraseology of that last sentence. It had, to his newly-sensitive ear, a slightly policeman-like ring. But the man seemed friendly enough; and Chalky could not believe that those kids had brought him here last night just to betray him. None of them seemed to be that type — not even Maman, for all that she wanted nothing to do with him.

But it was all right, after all. Chalky bathed, and was fed; and as he ate, the man asked: "How can I best help?" The question did not seem to require a reply, for he immediately answered himself.

"You will wish to go to Spain, of course. Without delay. And, naturally, you will not know the way."

"I've got a map," Chalky said.

"Aha! Well, now, let us examine this map."

Chalky took his map pouch from his pocket and, pushing aside his coffee cup, spread the appropriate map on the table.

"I thought Carcassonne would be a good kicking-off place," he suggested.

"Pardon?"

"Carcassonne. I thought I'd head into the Pyrénées from Carcassone."

"Ah, yes. A good choice. Well now," the man said briskly, "you should take the train to Toulouse. From Toulouse to Carcassonne is another train journey. You had better board the train on the Vichy side of the demarcation line. That would be safer. Train? Ticket. We must procure a ticket."

He looked at Chalky with a new intensity in his gaze, and Chalky began to feel uncomfortable.

"Have you a jacket?" the man asked suddenly.

"Just what I've got on," Chalky said.

"Ah, yes. The uniform."

"I reckon it does still look like a uniform," Chalky had to agree.

"They are not uniform trousers," the man stated.

"No," Chalky said, and did not amplify his answer. He didn't feel that it was a good idea to go into details. If this man was not, after all, as friendly as he seemed — well, it would be a pretty poor show if the Duhamels got into trouble through him.

"You found another friend," the man said, nodding. Chalky liked the implications of that word, "another."

"They were good to me."

"But you are careful to say nothing that would identify them. That is good. Even so, it would be better to say that you stole the trousers."

"I'll remember," Chalky promised humbly.

"So they gave you trousers. Perhaps I might contribute the

jacket." And he presently produced a double-breasted suit coat which, Chalky noticed, had had all possible means of identification cut from it. It did not match Monsieur Duhamel's trousers, though it was within cooee of the colour range. It was a bit on the tight side, especially across the shoulders, but not too much so, and Frenchman often seemed to wear clothes that fitted snugly, Chalky had noticed. At all events, the coat would not make him conspicuous. On the contrary, it would camouflage him more than adequately.

"I could do with a pair of boots or shoes," Chalky suggested. "Size eleven,' he added hopefully.

The man raised an eyebrow and shook his head.

"So large."

Chalky nodded. "I've got ingrown toenails," he explained. "Flying boots aren't meant for hiking in. They're giving me hell."

"A condition of the most painful," the man agreed sympathetically. "We shall see what can be obtained."

Chalky surveyed the double-breasted jacket, quite delighted with it.

"Are you sure you can spare it?" he asked.

The man shrugged carelessly. "But of course. It is quite old."

"It's in good nick," Chalky said.

"Pardon?"

"The jacket. It's in good condition."

The man shrugged again. "It is out of fashion."

"Fashion! My father's a farmer, and in all the years I've known him, he's only had one suit. It's his Sunday best. He wears it when he goes to town, to church, to the races, weddings, that sort of thing."

"It is sufficient," the man said. "I am in business, however, in Paris. A suit is my... how do you say? ... my working wear."

"Paris? Then this isn't — yours?" Chalky asked, waving a hand at his surroundings.

"But yes! I am come down from time to time before the war. Now I stay here mostly. Paris is no longer... pleasant. The Boche —. It is hard to bear, my friend, seeing those...

cochons ... strutting in our streets, hearing their barbaric language —"

"I can understand that," Chalky said.

"Can you? But — yes, perhaps you can. You have come a long way to fight them." The man looked at Chalky curiously. "Have you ... shot many of them down, the Boche?"

"A couple. I got those on the last trip, before they shot me down. And," he said, a certain simple satisfaction in his voice, "I knocked down a guard and got away from the bastards."

"Knocked down a guard! Tell me, Chalky —" it was the first time that he had used the nickname "— for how long were you a prisoner-of-war?"

"About three quarters of an hour."

The man stared, then laughed.

"Bravo!" he applauded.

He was instantly serious again.

"We must waste no time." He seemed, now, to be speaking to himself rather than to Chalky. "Ticket. We will purchase a ticket from Reuilly. From Reuilly to Toulouse. I will arrange it. Now — have you money for the journey?"

"Yes,"

"You will need bread coupons —"

"I've got a few."

"You had better have more. Who knows how long it will be before you can cross the Spanish frontier? Now, what more do we require?"

"I've got an identity card," Chalky said, "but it's not stamped."

The man nodded. "Give it to me. Sometimes it is possible. I will try what can be accomplished."

When Chalky had finished eating, and had stood up from the table and dressed himself in his now almost complete civilian outfit, he was conducted back towards the stable. The man bade him wait outside, while he himself went in, presently to emerge with a hoe in his hand. He led Chalky to a large vegetable garden.

"You will hoe some cauliflowers," he said. "It is better than hiding in the stable. If the Germans come, the stable they will search, and the house. But a peasant hoeing cauliflowers they will not even see."

Then off he went, to "try what could be accomplished."

He was gone for nearly three hours. When he returned, he had Chalky's rail ticket, for which he would accept no payment. But he had met with no success in trying to obtain a pair of size eleven boots, and neither had he been able to get Chalky's identity card stamped. But he had brought with him another man, a somewhat taciturn peasant, who was, nevertheless, friendly enough; and both men were wheeling bicycles.

"This is my bailiff," said Chalky's host.

"Pleased to meet you," Chalky responded, and put out his hand. The bailiff took it in his equally massive paw, and there was a brief and not very earnest test of grips. Then they both grinned faintly at each other and let go.

"He will take you to Reuilly."

Chalky resumed his jacket and when he was dressed, and had picked up his canvas bag, the man handed him his bicycle, and took his hoe as if in exchange. As he did so, he looked at the cauliflower patch, and then at Chalky.

"What do you do?"

"Eh?" The question took Chalky by surprise, and he hesitated for a moment, not quite sure what the question meant. Then there flashed into his mind a memory of Godefroi, in the Duhamel's cottage, asking the same question. He recalled that his answer had won Godefroi's acceptance, and he thought that perhaps it was something which would help establish him in the bailiff's favour, also.

"You said that your father was a farmer. Were you, also, a farmer?"

"Well, yes —" Chalky began. He wondered how to explain to a Frenchman the difference between a farmer and a farm contractor.

The man looked at the bailiff, who looked at the cauliflower patch, tossed his head and walked away.

"I should give it up," the man advised, not cracking a smile. "You will fail at it. You must be the laziest hoer in the world." Chalky thought, "Don't you worry, mate. I'd have hoed like the clappers if the Germans had come along."

"Come," said the bailiff. "I will take you to Reuilly."

"I can only say, thanks very much," Chalky looked at his host. "I don't even know your name."

"It is better that you do not," the man said, and the bailiff nodded. His name, as it happened, was Tissier, but Chalky did not learn that until some time later.

They cycled away from the farm, to all intents and purposes two beret-wearing Frenchmen going about their lawful business. When the bailiff waved to passers-by, Chalky waved also. It was always good camouflage, he thought, to appear to be part of the every-day scenery.

The way took them through leafy lanes and along country roads. The bailiff rode in the plodding fashion of the French countryman, unhurried but never freewheeling, pedaling at a pace which ate up the kilometres yet did not exhaust, or even raise a decent sweat. Time, Chalky reflected, seemed to mean nothing to the peasant; yet, in another sense, time meant everything. No one, not even the most harrassed businessman, had a greater respect for time than the peasant. Time, to the city dweller was always the enemy, because the city man tried to cram too much into a given measure. It gave him a jerky ride, therefore. But to the peasant, there were times and a time for performing all of life's various tasks and taking each of life's pleasures. Over the long ages, the tasks had been tailored to fit into the available time, so that each might be accomplished in its appointed season. Time moved to an unchanging rhythm, like the steady, plodding, unhurried revolutions of the pedals. And in the end, as the occasionally impatient Chalky had to admit to himself, they reached their goal with enough time in hand to preclude last-minute hustle and waste alike.

Before they parted, the bailiff went to the ticket office and enquired as to whether or not the train was running to time, which was a thoughtful thing to do; because the train was running late, about twenty minutes late, and might be expected at about half past two. Knowing this, Chalky wouldn't have to stand worrying over the delay.

There were no Germans in Reuilly, which, to Chalky's way of thinking, was a nice change. Of course, under the terms of France's surrender, as Chalky understood them, Vichy France was supposed to be Unoccupied France, a sovereign state at peace with Germany. But victorious Huns were not famous for being over-scrupulous in their regard for treaty terms. And anyway, their presence could always be explained as the rightful and helpful presence of allies. At any rate, Chalky was under no illusions regarding them. There were, in his estimation, just as likely to be Gestapo train checks in Vichy France as in Occupied France. Caution was still necessary.

It is difficult, however, to maintain an attitude of extreme caution without becoming edgy. Caution becomes suspicion, and suspicion engenders nervousness. As the twenty minutes stretched to an hour, an hour and a quarter, two hours, Chalky came close to the point of fleeing from the station and out into the countryside.

Then a railway official, seeing him standing on the platform, came up to him.

"Est-ce que vous attendez le train à Toulouse, Monsieur?"

Chalky recognised the word "Toulouse," and understood by the upward inflection at the end of the sentence that he was being asked a question. It wasn't difficult to deduce that the question concerned his desire to get to Toulouse.

"Oui," he said, trying to make the word sound as it did when the French said it.

"Il va arriver dans une demi-heure. Le délai est á cause du sabotage à la ligne."

It didn't take special genius to figure out what that was all about, either. *"Délai"* and *"sabotage"* and *"demi-heure"* and *"la ligne"* were all plainly recognisable words, adding up to the fact that the train was delayed a further half-hour, due to sabotage on the line. He nodded, shrugged, said *"Merci,"* and the man moved on.

The train, when it did arrive, was not very crowded. And when the guard came through to inspect the tickets, he was not accompanied by Germans. Chalky, therefore, sat back and surrendered his ticket in a comparatively relaxed and easy frame of mind.

"Il faut changer à Chateauroux," the guard said.

Chalky nodded. Again, it was not difficult to get the gist

of what was said. Chalky's ear for French was beginning to improve a little; and anyway, the bailiff had explained to him that he would have to change trains at Chateauroux.

There were Germans on the platform at Issoudun, but none, as far as he could see, embarked on the train. From Issoudun to Chateauroux, therefore, he was again able to relax and enjoy the ride.

It was strange, when he thought about it. Here he was, doing something which ordinarily was a rich man's activity — travelling in a foreign country. Ordinarily, few New Zealanders of his time ever left their own shores, and even fewer travelled to Europe. He supposed that he ought to be drinking in the scenery, dutifully enjoying the foreign landscape. But Chalky looked at it with a farmer's eye, and somehow it didn't look particularly foreign at all. There was the same pattern of green grass and autumn-ploughed, dark brown earth, and tawny stubble, and perfectly familiar trees. He could recognise the distant water courses just as he did at home, by the sinuous lines of willows. The sky was the same blue sky that he had always known. The clouds were the same clouds. Happily, too, there weren't many of them, and the weather remained benevolently fine. With that observation returned the full realisation of where he was, and why.

The journey from Issoudun to Chateauroux took just under an hour. By Chalky's map, the distance was about twenty-five kilometres, which should have been, at most, an easy thirty-minute run. He wondered if perhaps French railwaymen went out of their way to display their cussedness, to irritate the precision-minded Germans by not keeping even to their own timetables.

He stepped from the train at Chateauroux and made his way to the waiting room. He was beginning to dislike railway stations. It was so difficult, to sit around calmly, knowing that at any moment some curious French official might accost him; or, worse, that some German soldier or Gestapo agent might stand over him, blustering.

It wouldn't have been so bad, perhaps, if he had something to read, or if he could have gone and had a couple of beers somewhere. As it was, he just sat, pretending to read a newspaper, and making frequent trips to the toilet, not because he needed to, but just to relieve the anxiety a little by getting away out of sight for a while.

Sitting in the toilet, however, was just about as soul-destroying as sitting in the waiting room, and he considered going out into the town, to have a meal and a cup of coffee. But he didn't. The thing was, he told himself, that if you saw the occasional Hun on the railway station platform, you could be pretty sure of being hip-deep in them in town. It was better to stay where he was. And he did, for hours, until midnight, when his train departed for Toulouse.

Again, there were plenty of seats, and when Chateauroux was well behind him, and the guard had clipped his ticket, Chalky relaxed and dozed off. He half-awoke when the train stopped at Argentan, and the carriage doors were opened, and feet clattered up the aisle. Then, as the train moved off again, he sank into a deep sleep.

At about three o'clock in the morning, the train pulled into Limoges, and Chalky considered stepping down onto the platform to stretch his legs. He was warm and comfortable, however, and he dozed off again. This time he did not fall deeply asleep, and he was aware of much shunting and jerking and clattering; but he was sure that sooner or later the train would resume its journey.

He was awakened by the guard, who shook him and shouted in his ear:

"M'sieu'! Monsieur, s'il vous plait!"

"Eh?" Chalky said. Just in time he stopped himself from speaking in English.

"Monsieur, vous allez à Toulouse, n'est-ce pas?"

"Toulouse, oui," Chalky said, wide awake and apprehensive.

"Mais, monsieur, la rame de wagons qui va à Toulouse est parti! Cette rame est en route pour Bordeaux!"

"Bordeaux?" Chalky queried.

"La rame pour Toulouse est parti, monsieur," the guard repeated.

He kept pulling at Chalky's arm, and Chalky understood all at once that the train had been split — that this was what all the shunting had been about — and, as far as he could tell, this was the wrong portion. He assuredly did not wish to go to Bordeaux.

So there followed another of those long, aggravating waits, this time at Limoges. His dislike of railway stations blossomed into a remarkably foul mood. He hated railway stations. Railway stations stank with the sulphurous fumes of coal, and with tobacco, and with the sweat of generations of Frenchmen who, he told himself, waged perpetual war against any attempt to change the air in their vicinity. It was, he knew, no more true of the French than of train-travelling New Zealanders. You couldn't have windows open in coal-fuelled trains wending their way through close valleys and tunnels and the long cuttings of a hilly countryside; and because comparatively few people actually waited in waiting rooms, nobody ever bothered to open the windows, which would have been a futile exercise in any case, since they opened out onto the platform, and were there purely to allow passengers to keep an eye on the train while keeping smoke out of the waiting room. Chalky, knowing all this, still felt grumpy.

He tried to come to terms with this minor but irritating misfortune. At least, he reminded himself, he had plenty of food, plenty of bread coupons in case he should require more food, and sufficient money to pay for any additional food he might wish to buy. Grumpiness, however, is one of those ills of the spirit to which most of us are prone to cling until something happens along to beguile us out of it. In a perverse way, people rather enjoy being grumpy. They can get things off their chests, for one thing, which they would ordinarily bottle up. And Chalky did. He addressed the blind, closed ticket windows, and the fly-spotted light bulbs, on a variety of grievances, mostly concerning the Germans, the Huns, and their fitness for inclusion in decent human society.

Chalky had no way of getting his frustrations off his chest in any meaningful way. Swearing at the light bulbs was all very well, but it wasn't enough. He didn't speak French, and he didn't speak German; and if he had, he could hardly have gone up to one of the objects of his displeasure and told him how browned off he was with all this hiding and skulking jiggery-pokery. Accordingly, he had his swear at the furnishings of the waiting room, and then sat there and fumed, which at least squeezed from the forefront of his mind all thoughts of being picked up by the police or the Gestapo. And at last, after many hours, he boarded a train for Toulouse and resumed his journey.

There was a German train check on this one. When they entered the carriage there were few other passengers, and therefore no choice of slipping out to the toilet unnoticed. These were not Gestapo, however, but a stolid *Wehrmacht* corporal and two bored privates; Chalky felt a bit more confident than on previous occasions. In his civilian getup, he saw no reason why they should be suspicious of him — until they saw his unstamped identity card. He had to avoid showing that at all costs. Yet, a covert glance told him, they were checking the identity cards of the other passengers.

There was only one thing to do. Chalky lay back in his seat and feigned sleep.

He heard jackbooted feet come to a halt beside him.

"Presentez votre ticket et votre carte d'identité, s'il vous plait, monsieur," a voice said. His ticket was clamped loosely between the interlocked fingers of his hands, which were clasped comfortably over his stomach. He did not stir.

"Votre ticket et votre carte d'identité!" the voice said, more sharply. For effect, Chalky snored.

A hand touched his shoulder tentatively.

"Monsieur?"

He snored again and expelled air through his partly closed lips, and settled more comfortably in his seat. The ticket was deftly twitched from between his fingers.

"Gib ihm einen fusstritt," a bored voice said.

"Wir sind nicht in der Franzoschen Bestatzung zone," the first voice said sharply.

"Wir können keine zeit an ihm verschwende," a third voice said from farther down the carriage. *"Wir müssen mit der kontrolle fertigsein bevor Brive."*

"Ja, gut. Lass ihn sicher ist eine grenzkontrolle in Toulouse," the bored voice said. The ticket was pushed into his breast pocket and the feet clumped away.

German spoken often falls familiarly on the English ear. It required no great mental effort on Chalky's part to figure that they were in a hurry to complete their check before the train arrived at Brive, and were leaving him to be checked out by the barrier control at Toulouse.

Happily, again, there was no barrier control. Arriving in Toulouse in the early evening, he took a tram to the outskirts, where once again he chose a prosperous-looking house and asked for help.

The people were nervous, but did not refuse assistance.

"It is very dangerous, to keep you here," the man said in passable English. Having suggested the possibility — having, as it were, committed himself to the proposition that he was willing to help within limits, the man plunged a little further. "Possibly we can hide you, but it is best that we do not do so here. There are reasons —"

They gave him a good, hearty meal, and while he ate, the man left the house. It was Chalky's turn to become nervous.

But there was no need. The man returned again just as Chalky was finishing his meal. He was still alone. No gendarme was with him, and a covert glance through the window at the street showed that neither was there a car, or any sign of lurking men.

"There is a place for you to hide," the man promised, and Chalky heaved a sigh of relief.

"Let's go," he said. "The sooner I'm off your premises, the better."

But it seemed that the man was not coming with him.

"You must walk along that road," he said, pointing in the direction of the street. "It will take you out into the country." He explained to Chalky that he had obtained permission for him to sleep at a farmhouse, and told him how to find it.

A two kilometre walk brought Chalky to the place, a picturesque, white-walled building, well off the road, sitting amongst its orchards and gardens. The farmer, too, seemed more than a little nervous, and Chalky was not invited into the farmhouse, but was conducted to a shed, a lean-to structure against one wall of the house, wherein his bed was to be a pile of sacks.

"Still," he told the uncomprehending farmer, whose English was, to say the least, basic, "still, it's a bed, and it sure beats sitting around all night in station waiting rooms."

The farmer looked at him blankly, and shrugged. At the shed door he turned, and said, "When day come, you go." Then he left, shutting the door behind him.

True to the agreement, Chalky crept quietly away at daybreak, and walked back towards the outer suburbs of Toulouse. As he walked, he heard aero engines, and was intrigued to see, above the treetops, German FW190 fighters practicing climbing turns in this supposedly neutral piece of French sky. In spite of everything, Chalky was still a fighter pilot. He took careful note of their direction from the city; and then he walked on. He caught an early tram back to the city centre, to the railway station, where he purchased a ticket to Carcassonne, only to find that he had missed the early train, and would have to wait — in the bloody railway station, he told himself savagely — till four o'clock. Someone ought to pay for this! He was bolder, now, about such matters as buying tickets. He would simply walk up to the ticket window, spread his money on the counter, and demand: *"Troisième classe à Carcassone."* He figured that if his accent was wrong, the French would put it down to his being German, and any German who might overhear him would attribute it to his being provincial French. Mostly, he now suspects, the French recognised him as being British as soon as he opened his mouth to utter anything more than the odd monosyllable, it being well known throughout Europe that the British spoke other European languages with the most atrocious accent of all.

When, at four o'clock that afternoon, his train pulled out of Toulouse, he found that it was rather more full of Germans than was entirely comfortable, but in his current browned-off mood, he didn't care all that much. Nevertheless, caution did not forsake him entirely. He decided not to ride the train right into Carcassonne, but to leave it at Pezens, a village about five kilometres from that ancient city.

It is interesting, in retrospect, to record that this was a most fortunate decision. At the time, Chalky did not, could not, appreciate just how fortunate it was. He made it purely to save the trouble of having to take a tram straight out to Carcassonne's outskirts.

The fact was, Carcassonne was alive with Germans.

There are really two cities of Carcassonne. The original Carcassonne was a medieval walled city. Sometime in the nineteenth century, it was restored to its original splendour, and still, today, stands stabbing at the sky with its candle-snuffer turrets, and enwraps itself secretively within crenellated walls. Modern Carcassonne was once the village which huddled at the walled city's feet, close at hand, so that its inhabitants could take ready refuge within those formidable walls. And formidable they were, and are. England's Black Prince once turned prudently away from them, and carried his conquests elsewhere. The old place is still called the *Cité* of Carcassonne, to distinguish it from the newer town on the banks of the River Aude. The modern town is called the *Ville Basse*.

The Germans evidently found it a formidable stronghold, also. Already, in 1943, fearing an Allied invasion via the South of France, they had expelled the inhabitants from the *Cité*, walled up all but one of its great gateways, tunnelled under its priceless buildings to make bombproof bunkers, and established an important headquarters there, from which to command and deploy the increasing number of German troops moving into areas around the Golfe du Lion. Carcassonne, as Chalky White approached it all unaware, was a German town.

But at Pezens, he left the train. A small village, Pezens lay dozing in the last of the sunshine, amid vast acreages of the famous vineyards of Languedoc, and Chalky walked through it without seeing a soul. A little distance down the Carcassonne road, he saw a large house, almost a chateau, he reckoned, and he decided to go up to it, in the hope that its owners spoke English and would be disposed to help him. Remembering, however, that the chateau at Touffreville had been occupied by Germans, he approached this one carefully, through the vineyards, hiding amongst the vines and enjoying a feed of ripening grapes while he spied on the house, and observed the comings and goings.

Not that there were many comings and goings. The only

sign of life appeared to be the movements of a not over-energetic group of workmen, who seemed to be bringing in their tools preparatory to knocking off for the day; and he decided to go up to them and try their disposition.

He emerged from between the rows of vines and walked steadily enough up to the house, across a kind of yard surrounding by small buildings and shelters. The workmen appeared to be putting their tools away, and shrugging into their coats. They all turned and eyed him silently. He stopped a few paces from them, and they said nothing, but waited for him to speak.

They waited and he waited; and at last, feeling that someone had to make a beginning, he took his wings and flashes from his pocket.

It was an incredibly difficult thing to do, he found. He was so close to the Spanish frontier and success that he was loth to do anything that might put him at risk, that might once again make him a prisoner in this Hun-dominated country. But he did it. He opened his hand and displayed his wings and flashes.

"RAF," he said. "Does anyone here speak English?"

Nobody spoke. They came to him, one by one, and silently gathered around him, and looked at his wings; and one man poked at them tentatively with a grimy forefinger, then withdrew his hand and looked into Chalky's face.

"Attendez," he growled. He said something to one of the others, who looked for a long moment at Chalky, then moved off.

"Look," Chalky said, "if you can't help, OK. I'll just be on my way."

"Attendez," the man said.

There were too many of them to take on, Chalky thought. So he seated himself on a low stone wall and looked at them, and waited. And they stood around him in a semi-circle, not speaking, not even smiling when he smiled at them — and they, too, waited.

8.

After about half an hour of this, Chalky got tired of looking at those expressionless faces, and turned to gaze out across the darkening vineyard, to look somewhat longingly at the Carcassonne road. He wondered if he could get away from them at a fast sprint. But even as he looked, a car appeared from the direction of Pezens. He tried to discern, in the failing light, whether it was a German car, or a French police car, but he couldn't see it clearly enough. He rather hoped that it might drive on by, but it didn't. It turned in at the gateway and climbed up the driveway towards the house. As it drew closer, he saw, to his relief, that it was a slightly battered, very dirty Citröen with a monstrous gas producer belching out clouds of black smoke from its rear end. It had, he now saw, only one occupant, a jaunty young man in a slightly loud pinstripe suit and a black beret.

The Citroen ground to a halt in the yard. Its driver got out and, after a brief word with one of the workmen, walked straight across to Chalky.

"Anglais?" he asked.

Chalky nodded.

"RAF?"

"Yes," Chalky said.

The man put out his hand in a "give-me" gesture. When Chalky appeared nonplussed, he did it again. Chalky realised that he was being asked for his credentials. He dipped a hand into his pocket, watched closely and tensely by the man, whose own hands stole around the waistband of his pants, under his jacket, in what might have been a trouser-hitching movement if they hadn't stayed there. Chalky guessed that he was armed. He brought forth his wings and flashes and displayed them, and the man, after a moment, grinned beneath his pencil-line moustache, and nodded.

"OK. You come."

Chalky stood up and looked at the workmen.

"Thanks very much," he said. *"Merci beaucoup."*

For the first time, they smiled, and he shook hands all round.

"OK," the driver said, a note of impatience in his voice.

Chalky slung his overcoat and canvas bag into the back seat of the Citroën and climbed in. The man switched on, and the engine purred to life. He took a delicate finger-and-thumb hold on the gear lever, which protruded from the dashboard, let in the clutch, and they rolled smoothly down the drive and out onto the road.

At first they headed back towards Pezens, but turned off at the outskirts and drove in a cloud of dust down a very second-class road, into a winding valley.

Just below the town, they pulled into a driveway, and lurched along a farm track, curving around the shoulders of the gentle hills.

So far, the man had not spoken again; but after a while, Chalky, wishing to make the most of this chance of some English conversation, asked: "Where are we going?"

"You will see," the driver said. The way in which he said it made it obvious to Chalky that this was a conversational dead end. After a minute or two he tried again.

"She runs very smoothly," he said, reaching out a hand and patting the door sill.

"Oui."

"Engine sounds sweet as a nut," Chalky persisted.

"Oui."

"I always thought they ran pretty rough on these gas producers," Chalky said patiently.

The man gave a mouth-only grin, his expressionless eyes fixed on the worsening track ahead.

"Not on gas producer. German petrol. Gas producer camouflage."

"German petrol!"

"Oui."

"Oh."

After a long pause, the driver said, "Is possible to buy, you got money enough. Got money enough, buy anything."

"Even German petrol?"

"Oui. Even German petrol."

The car lurched sharply left past a clump of trees, bounded over a short saddle and slithered to a halt in a cloud of dust and gravel before a farmhouse nestled snugly in a fold in the hills, surrounded by its orchard and outbuildings.

The driver climbed out.

"OK," he said. "You come."

They entered the house, stepped from fading twilight into a cool, dark kitchen. As they came in and the driver shut the door, a match flared, and another, and two kerosene lamps were lit on a long kitchen table. In the growing light Chalky saw several other men sitting on plain wooden chairs about the room, drinking wine.

"Sit there," the driver said, indicating a chair at one end of the table. He himself sat at the other end. He reached behind him, under his coat, and pulled forth a huge revolver, which he placed somewhat ostentatiously on the table. Someone produced a bottle of Scotch and some glasses, which the driver filled and pushed one down to Chalky. He raised his glass, said *"Santé,"* and drank.

Chalky raised his own glass, said: "Up your kilt," and drank.

"The English," the driver remarked, "say, 'Cheerio.'"

"Some of 'em," Chalky agreed.

"All the English I 'ave ever meet say 'Cheerio,'" the driver said firmly.

"Some say 'Cheers,'" Chalky told him flatly. He wasn't sure that he liked the driver all that much.

"Cheerio," the driver insisted.

"Some say 'Down the hatch,' and some say, 'Mud in your eye,'" Chalky told him.

"But you say "Up your kilt.' You are not English?"

"No," Chalky said. "I'm not English." He had read somewhere that when you give evidence in court, you should answer the question, and only the question, and avoid giving unasked-for information.

There was a restless stir around the room.

"But you are RAF," another man said gently. It was a silken, dangerous gentleness.

"That's right," Chalky took out his wings and flashes and spread them on the table like a hand of cards.

"New Zealand," the driver read. "But the RAF is English."

"British," Chalky said. "I'm British."

"I understand." The driver stood up and moved around the table to refill Chalky's glass, then returned to his chair and sat down.

"New Zealand has its own air force," he said.

"That's right," Chalky said. "The RNZAF."

"But you are in the RAF? *Santé.*"

"Hair on your chest." Chalky took a pull at the whisky.

"But you are in the RAF?" the Driver persisted.

"In a New Zealand squadron," Chalky explained.

"I do not understand. If the New Zealand Air Force 'as come to fight with the RAF, why are you in the RAF?"

"The RNZAF has its hands full in the Pacific, but they still contribute aircrews to the RAF through the Empire Air Training Scheme."

They filled Chalky's glass again.

"But you said you are in a New Zealand squadron."

"Look," Chalky said, "this is bloody good Scotch, but I'm as dry as a chip. Could I have something to quench my thirst?"

Someone filled a tumber with wine and handed it to Chalky. He was beginning to enjoy this interrogation, he decided. Very hospitable blokes, these Frenchmen. Even the driver wasn't too bad, once you got to know him.

"But you said you are in a New Zealand Squadron," the driver prompted.

"That's right."

"But not in the Royal New Zealand Air Force?"

"That's right," Chalky said. "RAF. Here's to us. Who's like us? Damned few, and they're all dead." He raised his glass, took a long pull at the wine, which cooled his throat, and chased it down with a slug of that remarkably good Scotch.

"Is that not — extraordinary?" the driver asked.

"No, not extraordinary. Why should it be extraordinary?"

"You say," the driver said carefully, playing with his revolver, "that you are a New Zealand pilot, in a New Zealand squadron, but not in the New Zealand Air Force."

"That's right. Why not? Look, on the Op. I was shot down on, we were working with a French Squadron. It wasn't in the French Air Force. It was in the RAF."

"I understand." The driver took a sip at his own whisky.

"Well, I'm bloody thankful for that," Chalky said. "I was beginning to think that I wasn't getting through to you." He refreshed himself with wine, with a Scotch chaser.

"Tell me," the driver requested, "about being shot down."

"What's to tell?" Chalky wondered.

"Where was it? When did it happen? What kind of operation were you on?"

"We were on bomber escort duty, close cover," Chalky said. "The target was a German airfield at Beaumont-le-Roger."

"Beaumont-le-Roger?"

"Yes."

"I understand. Proceed."

"We were jumped by the Huns. There must've been hundreds of the bastards," Chalky said. "There were only twelve of us."

"Only twelve?"

"Plus twelve French Spitfires."

"Against hundreds of the Boche?"

"Well, one hundred, anyway."

"Was that not foolhardy? Is the RAF so . . . weakened?"

"Don't you believe it." Chalky took another wine-and-Scotch. "We weren't expecting the entire bloody Luftwaffe to take us on. No, we've got plenty more Spits where ours came from. It's just that we've got a lot of territory to cover. We can handle Jerry, don't you sweat," He drank some more wine and swallowed the last of his whisky. Quite a jolly interrogation, really.

"But — twelve against so many! That's wasteful."

"They had fewer targets than we did. Anyway, I got two. They aren't so good, the bloody Luftwaffe."

"They shot you down," the driver reminded him.

"A fat lot of good it did 'em," Chalky said belligerently. "How's the bottle?" The subject was beginning to bore him.

"Well, it is true that they 'ave not capture you," the driver allowed.

"Oh, they captured me."

"They capture you? Then you 'ave escape from a prisoner-of-war camp?"

"Not bloody likely. They only had me for about three quarters of an hour." Chalky told them the story of the farmhouse near Le Havre, and the unhappy guard who liked the smell of his tobacco.

There was a longish silence.

"What 'appened after that?" the driver asked after awhile.

Chalky told them, careful to omit names and details of those who had helped him. They shouted with laughter at his account of hiding in the toilet from the Gestapo, and the driver nodded approvingly at the mention of the children and the Parisian farmer. Only once did he stop him to ask him a question.

"This chateau. Where is it?"

"I forget," Chalky said promptly.

The Driver stared hard at him for a moment, fiddling meaningfully with his monstrous revolver. After a moment, however, he smiled.

Suddenly he asked: "What is your weight?"

Startled at the apparent irrelevance of the question, Chalky none-the-less tried to answer.

"I don't know," he said. "I've been walking quite a lot. I was fourteen stone when I weighed myself last. Why?"

The driver sat back in his chair, smiling.

"All right, Chalky White, RAF," he said. "You seem to 'ave manage well enough by yourself. What do you want from us?"

"I want to cross the border into Spain," Chalky said decisively. "I need a guide. I need some food. Mostly I need boots or shoes." He explained about his flying boots and his ingrown toenails. For some reason that escaped him, this seemed to amuse them, especially the driver.

"They're no joke to me," he growled.

"Pardon," the driver said. "I do not joke about the toes,

which must be most painful. Is simply that we are an organisation, you understand. We 'ave 'elp Allied airmen and refugees. There are organisations of the most efficient all across France. Yet you —. 'Ere you come, by yourself, seeking 'elp from no such organisation until you are almost at the Spanish frontier. Only then do you seek us out — to ask us for — oh, my friend, *mon cher ami* — for shoes for the easing of the feet!"

They all laughed, and the driver, who, as Chalky now perceived, was really quite a decent bloke, gave him another shot of that delectable Scotch and, when Chalky had swallowed it, another chaser of wine.

"The question is," Chalky said, returning to a state of solemnity, "the question is, can you do it?"

"The question is," the driver said, "not can we, but *when* can we? These matters must be adequately arranged."

He looked at his glass, and then at Chalky again. "In about a week."

"A week!"

"In about a week," the driver repeated. "Meanwhile, we will 'ide you."

"Here?" Chalky asked hopefully. In his present frame of mind, it seemed a splendid idea, to spend a week in this hospitable house amongst these terrific and understanding chaps. "I must say I'd be glad of a spell," he told them.

"Not 'ere. There is a farm, back in the 'ills, near Arfons,"

And so there was. In the darkness, the driver left Chalky there, promising to come back in about a week. Before he left, Chalky asked him the question which kept pushing its way to the forefront of his mind.

"What made you decide that I was OK?"

"Your weight," the driver said. "A German would 'esitate, try to convert kilograms to pounds. Stones 'e would not even think of."

He drove off, leaving Chalky with the feeling that these were formidable people indeed.

When he had gone, the farm people gathered Chalky into their circle. There was a French family, Parisians, mother and daughter. Father was absent, having been arrested in Paris and taken away by the Germans. Chalky could guess what for, because even here they were hiding two Jewish girls, one of whom was dark and attractive. Her name was Hanni. All spoke English.

The farmhouse was pleasantly hidden in a tree-shaded hollow. Two-storeyed, its lower floor served as both barn and cow-byre, which, as Chalky discovered, lent a homely tincture to the atmosphere of the living quarters on the upper floor. It was not unpleasant, being a warm and webby smell, slightly dusty and somewhere between a cow's clover-sweet breath and new-mown hay.

For Chalky it should have been a restful time, and in some respects it was. He was able to operate on his toenails sufficiently to give his feet a little much-needed relief. And it wasn't only his toenails that were painful. Nobody who has not tramped a considerable distance in fleece-lined boots can possibly know just what they can do to the feet. Firstly, the wool compacts, making a lot of unwanted space within the boot, causing it to flop about on the foot. Secondly, compacted wool is lumpy, creating numerous pressure-points, which give rise to callouses and raw patches. Thirdly, the feet sweat, causing scalds between the toes. Chalky padded about the house barefoot, and presently Madame found for him a pair of *espadrilles,* sandals made of rope and fastened with thongs, which at least kept his feet cool, and allowed the raw patches to heal. He soaked his feet, spread his toes with wads of cotton wool, massaged his maltreated insteps, trimmed away calloused skin and corns.

But one thing he did not do, that instinct warned him not to do, was to sit around, idle. He kept himself busy, because empty days are an opiate, drugging and dulling the mind and sapping the will; and Chalky had not yet accomplished his purpose. The hardest part, the crucial part, had yet to come. In any case, he was not made for idleness. Therefore he busied himself. The farm people made cornflour for their bread with a heavy stone grinder which they operated laboriously by hand, as probably a hundred generations of farmers in these brown and rounded hills had done before them. But these were Parisians, city people, unused to such tasks, and although they tackled them gamely and accomplished them successfully, these things were a burden. Sometimes, Chalky noticed, Madame would pause in the middle of some menial task, look at her ruined hands, and sigh.

So Chalky took over the grinding. He was powerfully, muscularly fit, yet he said afterwards that it was the hardest, heaviest work he had done in a long time. He ground as much as he could, so that they would have a reserve, be ahead of the game, able to do a little less each day and still keep the supply topped up.

And he milked the cow. He didn't know how they went about the task, but he was used to doing it in a particular way. With some lumber, he fashioned a bail, behind which he piled a supply of hay. The cow was persuaded to put her head through it to feed on the hay, Chalky closed the bale so that she couldn't get out again, and he leg-roped her. The family giggled amusedly when he sat himself on a stool, bucket tilted forward between his feet, his head resting against her flank, and reached flexing fingers towards her udder. And they murmured in polite wonder, and squealed and laughed in bright astonishment as the milk jetted into the pail.

"We could not believe," Hanni, the Jewish girl, said when presently he presented them with the warm and foaming milk. "We could not believe that you could milk a cow!"

"Why not?" Chalky wondered, grinning. "Nothing to it."

"But —" Madame said hesitantly.

"But what?"

"But — you are an *aviateur* — an airman. An RAF."

"Just for the duration," Chalky said.

"And you come from *Nouvelle Zélande!*"

"We've got cows in New Zealand," Chalky assured her. "I was milking three of 'em at the age of five."

Madame nodded. "Of course. One should have known. It is just that — sometimes the war — it seems to have always been, you understand."

"I know what you mean,"

"Do you? I wonder —"

"Yes," Chalky said, "I know. It's hard to remember what it was like before, even for me. It's a lot harder for some.

We've got kids in the Squadron who were at school when it started. They've never had another job, some of them. By the time they were old enough to drink, to smoke a cigarette, these things were rationed. By the time they were old enough to drive, or earning enough to afford a car, petrol was rationed. Me, I've been around a bit. But them —. The first job they've ever had was to go flying against Huns. Yeah, I reckon I know."

"Yes," Hanni said positively, "you know. These things I think of, also. They took my parents and my grandparents. All my friends are gone."

"All arrested?" Chalky asked. He nearly said, "All in concentration camps?" But he stopped himself in time. She knew well enough what the arrest of Jews meant. She didn't need reminding.

"I do not know," Hanni said. "Some have been . . . helped . . . the fortunate ones, the ones with good friends —" She put her arm about Madame, who placed her arm about Hanni's shoulders and smiled at her. "Some," Hanni went on, "have escaped." She looked at Chalky for a moment, oddly, as though sizing him up.

"I have one very good friend in England," she said. "She escaped to England before the fall of France." She told Chalky her friend's name. "If I give you her address," she requested, "would you tell her that I am safe?"

"Be glad to," Chalky promised. "If you'll just jot down her name and address —"

"No!" Hanni and Madame spoke together. Then, more gently: "No," Hanni said. "It is not safe. If you are caught, and they find on you her name, they will ask questions. They will require you to tell them from whom you obtained this name and address . . ."

"The Gestapo," Chalky nodded. "I reckon you'd be right. OK, well, look, you tell me, and I'll commit it to memory. The Huns can't see what's written in my head."

Hanni rehearsed him in her friend's name and address daily; and daily he ground flour and milked the cow. Then, early one morning, the driver came for him. He arrived at the farm, this time in a small Fiat car.

"It is time," he said simply. "Bring your belongings."

Chalky didn't need to be told twice. He said his goodbyes, dutifully repeated for Hanni her friend's name and address, and climbed into the car.

The driver took him back to the first farmhouse, near Pezens, where he had been interrogated; and here he was issued with an MAS-35 automatic, with the laconic instruction, "Shoot first and ask questions later." Thinking of Hanni and what she had been through at the hands of the Hun, he found it to be advice that suited his mood and his temperament. The driver also gave him a small, oblong package.

"Whatever happens, do not lose it," he requested.

"She'll be right," Chalky assured him as he stowed it in his canvas bag. On an impulse, mischievously, he asked with studied innocence what the package contained. The driver ostentatiously failed to hear the question. A smuggler, Chalky decided. That's why he's going over the Spanish frontier. That's why he has at least two cars. That's why he's into the black market racket that gets him German petrol, and a new pinstripe suit in a country where new clothes are obviously hard to get.

They wasted no time at the house, but got back into the little car and drove through Pezens at a moderate, entirely lawful pace, a gas producer almost as big as the car itself smoking furiously. They did not take the Carcassonne road, but instead crossed the River Aude and headed south. Presently they turned eastward, onto the Carcassonne-Montréal road, leaving it again about a kilometre farther on, and heading south once more, through Arzens to Cepte, where they joined the Carcassonne-Perpignan highway, a broad, paved road which took them through Limoux and Quillan. Soon after leaving Quillan, they turned south, winding and climbing into the mounting foothills of the Pyrénées.

Until now the driver had spoken seldom, except to name the odd town as they passed through, or to point out buildings or features as one does when showing the countryside to a visitor for the first time. As the road swung around beneath the Pic Madres and ran into the little town of Formigueres, however, he broke his near silence.

"About ten kilometres ahead," he told Chalky, "is the Forbidden Zone. We 'ave to pass a German control point."

"Will there be any — bother?" Chalky asked.

"Bothair?"

"Will there be any trouble?"

The driver shrugged. "Per'aps. I do not know. I am known there by some Germans. I 'ave choose this route because there is no town where the road crosses the demarkation line. Soldiers at such a post are bored. Is easy to make the friendly conversation. And they get careless. Also, sometimes one may do a little... business with them. Bring back small luxuries. It is for them... it is —"

"One of the perks of the job?" Chalky suggested.

"Perks?"

"Privileges," Chalky said after some thought. "Little extras that the job gives you."

"*Ah, oui!* Perks, ha ha!" The driver was instantly serious again.

"Is possible," he said, "that one of my... friends — will be on duty. Then, I think, we will 'ave no difficulty. In any case, I 'ave a pass, a permit of the police, to go into the Forbidden Zone. If I say, simply, that you are my partnair, per'aps it will suffice. But if the guard does not know me, my pass will be sufficient; but for you he may be — difficult."

"Is there much chance of that?" Chalky wanted to know.

The driver shrugged and said nothing. After a few moments, just as Chalky was on the point of asking what he should do, the driver asked, "You 'ave your pistol?"

Chalky patted his jacket pocket, which bulged with the weapon.

"Is loaded?" the driver asked, even more pointedly.

"Is it —?" Suddenly, Chalky understood. He took the weapon from his pocket and turned it over in his big hands. There was a long, knurled lever above the trigger which he took, rightly, to be the safety catch. Beneath it, at the base of the trigger guard, he discovered a knurled knob, which he pressed experimentally. The magazine promptly slid from the butt. It was fully charged. He slammed it home again, flipped off the safety catch and worked the sliding jacket. A round jumped out and fell into the back of the car. He felt a fresh one slide into the chamber. He clicked on the safety catch again and placed the weapon on the seat, under his right knee.

"It's loaded," he said.

They crossed a bridge, climbed a steepish, more or less straight stretch of road which ran diagonally up a precipitous face and swung around the point of a long spur. Down into a deep valley they went, and up over a saddle, from the top of which Chalky could plainly see, on a flat terrace below, a long, low, wooden building beside which stood a smaller, detached building like a toll booth.

"Hope that it is my friend," the driver said.

It was not his "friend." It was a hard-eyed, by-the-book, keen young private, who grudgingly acknowledged the validity of the driver's Vichy Police pass, but who was decidedly sticky about Chalky. Chalky himself could not understand the rapid exchange of French, but it was easy enough to guess, from the gestures, and from the tentative steps the soldier kept taking towards the car, that he was likely to be unceremoniously yanked from his seat and made to give a proper account of himself, or else. The German fended the driver's clutching hands and took two sideways steps towards the car, arguing furiously. The driver seized his arm and made what sounded like a passionate plea, releasing the German in order to stab at the dial of his wristwatch with an agitated forefinger. The German took two more steps. The driver tried once more to restrain him. The German's voice began to rise. Chalky took the automatic from beneath his leg, held it with both hands, resting it upon the car's window sill, and fired, three times. It took three shots. The MAS-35 was notorious for the lightness of its load. The German fell, the driver leaped for the car and tumbled into the seat. There was a trampling of feet from within the long building, and a certain amount of shouting, drowned all at once by the furious revving the little car's engine. The driver let in the clutch, the car almost stalled, there was a scream of spinning tyres, and off they went like a rocket. Chalky, looking back, saw two men running towards the dead guard, and others beginning to lift rifles towards their shoulders. Faintly, as their Fiat slithered around a bend, out of sight of the check point, Chalky heard the long tearing of a Schmeisser. He turned and sat facing forward once again.

"Argumentative bastard." He felt somewhat shaken, never having shot a man at close range before.

"Good shooting," the driver said.

"Thanks."

"But not soon enough," the Driver said evenly.

"I didn't know what was going on," Chalky explained. "He might've let us through."

"Is look like he is letting us through?"

"How the hell would I know? I couldn't understand a word either of you were saying," Chalky said hotly.

"Ah, well —" the driver shrugged. He looked at Chalky and grinned. "In this business, we do not play games." He slowed the car and pulled off the road, following an unsuspected track into the tall scrub until the car was well concealed from the road.

"From 'ere," he said, "we walk. Bring the package. Do not lose it."

They walked out from the scrub, brushing the long grass upright again where their wheels had flattened it, and began to walk briskly along the road. It made Chalky somewhat uneasy, since he expected moment by moment that a German car would surely come hurtling around the corner behind them, in hot pursuit. But nothing came, and they walked along the road for about a kilometre before the driver condescended to return to the cover of the scrub.

They trudged over uneven ground, around steep shoulders and over ridges until at length they came close to the road again near the crest of a slight rise. The driver began to move with more caution, now, and Chalky took his cue from him. Near the crest, the driver stopped, and began to creep forward with infinite care, keeping behind screens of bushes as much as possible. And at last he stopped, and beckoned Chalky forward.

Below them, Chalky saw, was a bridge, and beyond the bridge, a village was half hidden in the trees.

"Mont-Louis," the driver said, pointing. "The road is run down to Bourg-Madame, on the French side of the frontier, and Puigcerda, which is frontier town. The German garrison which mans the post through which we 'ave pass is at Llivia, in that direction. They will know, by now, and be on the alert. I think that bridge down there is already be guarded."

It was a trestle bridge, with a superstructure of thick wooden beams which obscured the decking.

"I can't see any signs of life," Chalky said.

"Is hard to see in this light," the driver said. "They will be cautious. So will we. We go down quietly, after dark, and we shall see what is to be discovaired."

"Suits me," Chalky said. The driver was in charge. If he was a successful smuggler, he knew the score. Just the same, it was hard to wait, with Germans so close behind, and Spain so near.

So near?

"Where is the frontier, from here?" he asked.

"Almost ten kilometres — that way," the driver pointed. Following his finger, Chalky saw what seemed to be precipitous mountain walls.

"Which side of those mountains?" he asked with some misgivings. Perhaps the driver heard the doubt in Chalky's voice, for he looked at him searchingly in the failing light.

"On top," he said.

"Those are the Pyrénées?"

"What else?"

"We've got bumps on the road bigger than those, at home," Chalky said disparagingly, more as an encouragement to himself than as a put-down or a proud boast. At — he judged — between eight and eleven thousand feet, the Pyrénées were high enough, especially for a man half-crippled with ingrown toenails, and with *espadrilles* on his feet.

They waited for over two hours before the last light faded. There was no traffic on the road, and nobody had approached that bridge.

"Come," the driver said, and began to creep forward. He paused once to caution Chalky against making any sound, and together they worked their way down hill and across the river terrace, towards the bridge. They lay in the scrub about twenty-five yards from it, listening, straining their eyes for sight of any movement, but there was nothing.

"Perhaps we can —" the driver began to whisper; and in

that instant they both saw it, the faintest orange glow, just for an instant, on one of the timbers of the bridge parapet. A German sentry was risking a quiet cigarette....

9.

Chalky reached out to lay a precautionary hand upon the driver's sleeve in the same moment that the driver reached forth to lay a hand on his. Their knuckles met in the darkness with a crack which sounded to Chalky's super-sensitized ears like the Last Trump. Tensely the two men waited for a reaction from the bridge.

Nothing happened.

"Come," the driver whispered. He crept backwards from their place of concealment and moved off, bent double, through the scrub, away from the bridge. Chalky followed in some haste, anxious not to lose sight of his guide.

He needn't have worried. For one thing, the moon was beginning to rise, and off to their left its glow was already revealing the foothills through which they had come, irregular humps of blackness against a brightening sky, and the driver was not too difficult to see, even amongst the shadowy bushes. For another thing, Chalky was still carrying the parcel, and the driver had already indicated that he was not about to be separated from it by more than a yard or two.

They moved away, downstream from the bridge, for about two hundred yards, until the driver was persuaded that it was safe to cross the river. The spot he chose was not a ford, exactly, but it was not very wide, a mere eighteen or twenty feet, knee deep but swift, with its bottom strewn with cricket-ball-sized boulders which slid under the feet and punished the insteps. One thing became quickly apparent, and that was that it couldn't be crossed wearing *espadrilles* without a serious risk of breaking an ankle; so Chalky took the sandals off, tied them about his neck, and rolled his trousers up above the knee. The driver, ever prudent where his package was concerned, took it from Chalky and waded in. By the time Chalky had stepped gingerly into the icy water, the driver was half way across, and was turning and beckoning impatiently about every two paces. He once almost lost his own footing, and sloshed about noisily for a few seconds. Even so, it was not his splashing so much that alarmed Chalky, as the fact that beneath that lightening sky, with the rim of the moon now visible above the peaks of the foothills, the driver was so plainly visible.

They accomplished the crossing quite quickly, probably more so than it seemed. It possibly took no more than two or three minutes.

On the southern bank, the driver now gave the package back to Chalky. Chalky whispered aggrievedly, "I wouldn't've got it wet."

He sat down on the rank, whispy grass, put on his *espadrilles* and rolled down his trouser legs. Then he took up the parcel, and turned to face the mountains. The driver, placing a hand on his sleeve, whispered into his ear: "Is a road and railway. We cross these, and we commence our climb to the Spanish frontier. Just the road and the railway, my friend. Come."

They started forward, over the river gravel, which soon gave way to stony soil, and to grass which kept catching in the thongs of Chalky's *espadrilles* and dragging sharply and tormentingly across his toes, and sticks of dead, dry gorse which stabbed at his feet. And there, in front of them, almost at eye level, was the banked-up road, already a long, straight ribbon of moonlight.

They could see no one on it in either direction, but that meant nothing. Down towards the bridge there were trees, and the shadows of trees, and a battalion could have been lined up in column of fours along that stretch of road, and been quite invisible.

"Come," the driver whispered again. They scrambled up the low embankment and, one at a time, bent low, scuttled across the road, slithering down the embankment on the other side and squatting breathlessly in the long grass, listening.

There was no sound but the hushing of the breeze in the dry gorse, and after a moment or two they stood up. Thirty-odd yards away, a precisely similar embankment carried the railway, the tracks of which glinted in the brilliant moonlight. Between the two men and those tracks lay fields of potatoes, divided from each other by low stone walls.

They crept forward between clumps of straggling gorse and began to cross one of the potato patches, keeping close to the stone wall, stealing quietly towards the railway line. As they reached the foot of the embankment, they heard a voice, clear and close on the quiet air.

"Sie müssen dort durch die grenze," it said, *"da können wir sie festnehmen."* (They will have to cross, and then we will take them.)

The driver half-turned to Chalky and made a staying gesture with his hand. He began to ease himself up the embankment, on his stomach. But this embankment was pure shingle ballast, and stones rattled away from beneath his toes.

"Wer ist das?" a sharp voice called — from about twenty yards away, Chalky judged. (You develop an ear for distance early, when you've grown up riding around the ewes at lambing, alert for a ewe in difficulties in some hidden hollow.) The driver ducked his head down, but his involuntary stiffening dislodged stones in even greater volume, and he slithered backwards in a positive avalanche of gravel. There was another shout from down the line, and the night was suddenly ablaze with gunfire. Chalky threw himself down behind the wall, and the driver hurled himself backwards from the embankment and landed beside him.

"Merde!" he said violently. He tugged an automatic from the waistband of his pants, bobbed up and pumped a fast fusilade of shots in the direction of the Germans. There was an almost startled, instantaneous silence from their side, quickly followed by barked orders. From the top of the railway embankment, from the next-but-one stone wall and, more alarmingly, from the direction of the road, the shooting started again. Schmeissers, with a rate of fire that made them sound like the monstrously amplified tearing of calico, ripped out

No. 485 Sqn Spitfires set out on a sortie over France.

"... evidence of how successfully Chalky put it down on that French paddock." This photograph appeared in Flugsport, *a German aviation magazine, which did not tell its readers that Chalky not only escaped but also returned to England to fight again.*

M. & Mme. Duhamel, of the chateau near Touffreville. The photograph was taken when Chalky visited them after the Liberation.

Chalky being congratulated by F/O H.S. Tucker on his return to England from occupied Europe.

long bursts. Individual shots cracked overhead and thudded against the other side of the wall.

Again, the driver bobbed up and started shooting, spraying rapid fire into the night. Chalky, also, peered over the top of the fence and blazed away with his pistol. He figured that even if they weren't hitting anything, they were sure keeping up an impressive rate of fire. The Germans evidently thought so, also, for they made no attempt, for the present, to rush the position.

The driver ducked down and slammed another magazine into his shooter. Chalky squeezed off the last two rounds in his and did likewise. Bullets were thumping into the other side of the stone wall, and ricocheting off the top of it and whining and chirruping away into the darkness.

"Come!" the driver said urgently. He loosed off another five shots, tapped Chalky on the shoulder, and scuttled off across the field, bent double. Chalky wasted no time, but followed. They dived over the next wall, picked themselves up, crossed that field, rolled over yet another fence, and continued that awkward bent-over flight.

Chalky's feet were hurting badly, the *espadrille* thongs cutting into his toes, the rope soles slithering dangerously under him. He plunged on desperately after the driver — who suddenly disappeared.

Chalky hesitated for a split second. The thought flashed through his mind that he ought to stop and look for the driver. He was certain that his guide had been hit. Bullets were still chipping gravel from the embankment, and cracking about his head, and he decided that if he stopped to poke around amongst the potato plants he would be killed. He was moving even as he thought about it, and he decided that it would be better to gain the shelter of the next fence. From there, he could survey the field; and when he had spotted the driver, he could make straight for him and drag him to safety — if he were still alive. But he hesitated again, unable to move on without at least finding out whether the driver was alive or dead. In an agony of indecision, he took a pace or two, made to move on, stopped, stepped forward again — and was almost pulled off balance as a hand seized his leg from behind.

"Down!" the driver commanded urgently.

He dropped down, and they lay together, panting, hearing voices and occasional shots, seeing patrol cars speeding along the road with spotlights, and listening to the sounds of shooting and shouting at no very great distance down the railway line.

"We've got to get out of this," Chalky whispered. "They're trying to cut us off."

"Where is the package?" the driver wanted to know.

"Bugger your bloody package!" Chalky said hotly. "What are we going to do about them?" He waved a hand at the patrol cars, moving slowly, their spotlights criss-crossing as they swept the potato fields, and at the railway line, down which men were still shooting and calling to one another at no very great distance from where he lay.

"For the moment, nothing," the driver said.

"We can't stay here," Chalky protested.

"Quiet! Where is the package?"

"Here," Chalky said crossly. "Here's your damned parcel. Look, this is getting too dicy for me. Let's do something —"

"The moon is very bright," the driver pointed out. "If we move, they will see us."

"If we don't move soon," Chalky argued, "they will fall over us."

High in the velvet sky, there was just one, small, solitary cloud. Even as they watched, before their gladly incredulous eyes it began to slide across the face of the moon. For precious moments, the darkness deepened.

"Come," the driver said, adding, "and give me the package."

Chalky handed it over willingly, and followed the driver across the potato patch to the embankment. He glanced up at the moon apprehensively, but it was still hidden behind that single cloud. If it was unveiled as they were crossing the line, he thought, that would just about be it. In any case, even with its face covered, it still lit the sky to an alarming degree. They would probably be seen anyway. The Huns were going to get them for sure.

They did not cross over the line. The driver seized Chalky's arm, and together they plunged into a culvert beneath it. They splashed in the little runlet which it carried from some spring on the mountainside, and they slithered in the slime; but they got through to the other side. Half-running, they made their way up a steepish slope. It was the start of their climb into the Pyrénées.

The climb was difficult, doubly so for a man wearing *espadrilles*. The slopes were steep and stony; and they were still in French territory, with German patrols still shooting and yelling and making a considerable fuss in the valley not very far below.

That, of course, was reassuring. As long as the Huns were poking about down there, Chalky thought, it was all right with him. It might keep 'em busy for hours — keep 'em out of the pubs, he told himself, and a jolly good thing, too. But sooner or later, someone was going to notice that culvert, and Jerry would know that they had got across the railway line after all. Then there would be patrols coming into the mountains after them, they would be much better armed than Chalky or the driver, they would have boots which fitted their feet, and would be better equipped all round for this sort of caper. All things considered, Chalky felt, their best bet was to make straight for the top and down the other side. The top, according to the driver, was the frontier.

But although the top didn't seem all that far away when you looked at the range from down there in the valley, it was a desperately long way when you actually tried climbing to it. There were layers, as it were, of faces and ridges, and there were lateral spurs and deep folds, all of which added up to hours and hours of climbing.

The cloud had gone from the face of the moon, now, and the bright moonlight was a help rather than a hindrance. It helped them to see goat tracks and footholds, and to avoid difficult and dangerous places. But it was no assistance at all to the scurrying, shooting, thoroughly aroused Germans down on the railway, because it so picked out the open bush patches on the mountainsides, and patched the slopes with innumerable black shadows, that two men climbing were all but invisible.

They climbed for several hours while the moon sailed serenely across the cloudless sky, painting the jagged peaks of the central massif, around the 11,000 foot Maladetta, and making the nearer-at-hand, ancient rocks shine whitely. And at last, exhausted, knowing that they must rest, they scrambled onto the top of a huge rock from which they commanded a perfect view of the surrounding slopes, and took turns to sleep, about an hour each.

Not much refreshed, but with the ache in their legs and backs somewhat eased, they ate some bread and cheese, and continued their climb towards the top of the range.

The moon had set some time during their two hours' rest, and there was a stillness and an early morning chill in the air. It was a cold rather more intense, more bone-chilling, than Chalky had hitherto experienced on his odyssey, the combined effect of deepening autumn, increasing altitude, and tiredness.

Their exertions, however, warmed them, heated them, had them sweating as they skirted a large patch of bush and laboured up the slope. They reached a sort of shelf, where they were able, for a little distance, to walk upright and easily, and from here Chalky looked up to where the tops of the Pyrénées, something over 8,000 feet in this vicinity, leaned back against the starry sky, shadowy and indistinct. The frontier seemed a long way off.

They paused for a moment at the foot of the next slope, and the driver handed his precious package back to Chalky, who stowed it in his canvas bag, thinking as he did so that the driver must have decided that he was able to make it to the top after all.

"I reckon we're about a quarter of the way to the top," Chalky remarked. The driver grunted, and looked back, northward. His eyes roved along the rumpled landscape, indistinct in its pools of blackness, and he pointed wordlessly to the north-east. Chalky, looking, saw far foothills becoming sharp against a paling sky.

"Is necessary to hurry," the driver said. "Is soon be daylight."

He turned, and Chalky, after another glance at the first flags of dawn, and a quick peer downward into the winking darkness, turned to follow. They had climbed for about twenty or thirty feet when, shockingly close, they heard a dog bark.

"Stand!" the driver whispered urgently.

Chalky stood still, uncomfortable on a narrow step which felt like a sheep track beneath his painful feet.

"What is it?" he whispered. He knew what it was. He really wanted to know what it was doing there, and who it was with, but found it difficult to frame the question.

"Is a patrol, maybe," the driver said, confirming his worst fears. "S-h-h-h!"

The dog barked again. They stood, the early breeze making their sweaty clothing clammy against their skin. Listening tensely, they heard no footsteps, no rattle of disturbed stones on that precipitous slope, no orders or conversation, no rattle of arms and accoutrements, but only the hushing of the breeze about their ears and in the trees close by, and the frequently repeated bark of the dog, punctuated now with an impatient whining, as though it were imploring someone to come and see.

"We can't stand here all day," Chalky whispered.

"Let us go forward," the driver agreed. "With caution," he added unnecessarily.

They moved upwards nervously, ready for anything. The driver, Chalky suddenly noticed, had his automatic in his hand. Chalky, using one hand to assist him in his climbing and the other to keep pushing his canvas bag out of the way, left his pistol where it was, in his coat pocket.

"Stop!" the driver commanded suddenly. Chalky had already stopped. They had reached the lip of a hanging valley, and there, in front of them, faint amongst a clump of shadowy trees, was a small stone hut.

The dog, which Chalky could now see, was chained to a lean-to kennel by the hut's door. It was an enormous beast, not unlike a St Bernard, but leaner and possibly even bigger. It was barking and growling fiercely.

As the driver and Chalky crouched beside a rock, the door of the hut opened and a man appeared. As he held up a hurricane lamp, Chalky could see that he was as large and hairy and rough as his dog.

"Qui est-ce que?" they heard him ask. The dog, peering through the half-light at the rock, gave a long, rumbling growl and barked again.

"That's no German," Chalky whispered.

The driver nodded, and climbed to his feet, holding his automatic behind his back.

"Nous dirigeons vers Espagne," he said. *"Nous n'y entendons pas malice."*

The man eyed him silently for a moment. Then: *"Il y avait l'action, là-bas,"* he said, pointing down into the dark sea of shadow below them. The driver gave a mirthless, hard bark of laughter which he probably intended to sound carefree.

'On nous a manqués," he said, repeating in English for Chalky's benefit: "They missed us."

"Nous?" the man queried.

"Stand up," the driver instructed Chalky. To the peasant he repeated, *"Nous."*

"What's he saying?" Chalky asked.

"He is say he hear the shooting down in the valley," the driver explained, "and I say they are trying to shoot us, and he is ask how many of us there are, and I show him there are only two of us."

"Avancez-vous," the man said, beckoning with one hand. The other hand, Chalky noted apprehensively, was on the collar of the large dog, as if ready to release it. But as they approached, his hand slid up from the collar to the head of the rumbling creature. The rumbles subsided, and it sat, very still, its body in a position of submission but its expression, Chalky felt, full of canine disapproval. As the driver drew up to the door, the man placed a hand upon his shoulder.

"Entrez," he invited. He placed his hand upon Chalky's shoulder and repeated the invitation. The dog's long, curving tail gave a niggardly two or three sweeps across the beaten earth.

Inside the hut, a woman had lit a kerosene lamp, and was carefully adjusting its wick. She smiled at them, a warm, almost motherly beam. Either she was abnormally trustful, or she had implicit faith in her man's judgement, Chalky thought.

Out there, beside the rock, he had drawn his automatic. Now he kept it behind his back, and he reached under his coat tail as if to hitch up his trousers, and unobtrusively tucked it into the waistband. The driver, however, kept his in plain view, dangling it negligently in his right hand until a glance into the farthest corners of the single room assured him that no one else was in the cottage. Then he tucked the weapon into the front of his pants, with its butt plainly visible.

The peasants appeared to disregard it, as if it were of no importance whatever.

"C'est ma femme," their host said. She bobbed her head and smiled.

It seemed that he was a shepherd. He looked the part, in his wide Basque beret and his sheepskin coat. He suggested that Chalky and the driver had better stay all day, resuming their journey in the evening, when darkness fell. They would, he promised, be perfectly safe. As he took his flock out, he would keep a watch for German patrols. If they came dangerously close, he would give a signal which his wife would recognise, and they would have plenty of time to get away.

They gave the two fugitives food and wine, and the shepherd and the driver engaged in pleasant conversation, while the shepherd's wife smiled at Chalky from time to time as she went about her various chores. Through the driver, the shepherd learnt that Chalky, also, had been a shepherd, and for a time they compared notes. Then it was time for the shepherd to take his sheep out to pasture.

"Where does he keep them?" Chalky asked the driver. He had seen no fences, no yards, no sheepfold.

"L'Anglaise a une question?" the shepherd asked.

The driver repeated Chalky's question to him French.

"Eh," the shepherd said. *"Monsieur, venez voir."*

He took from a peg on the wall a battered brass trumpet, and, beckoning to Chalky to follow, went outside. He loosed the dog, which stood at his side, looking at him expectantly. There, as the dawn scrabbled with cold fingers up the eastern sky, the shepherd placed the trumpet to his lips, took it away again, moistened his lips, took a deep breath, and blew two notes, which he repeated at intervals. Chalky watched him, wondering, until the driver, standing close by, touched him on the shoulder and pointed.

"Look," he said quietly, "there, and there, and there." And he pointed in turn to patches of bush, to rocky outcrops, and to folds and hollows about the stone hut.

All his life, Chalky will remember what he saw in that clear chill dawn light. It was strange. It was more than strange. In that place, on those mountains, in that clean, early light, sheep were emerging from the woods and outcrops and hollows. Silently, without bleating they came, walking placidly and without haste, filing along their own terraced tracks.

The shepherd placed the bugle to his lips again, and again blew, different notes, this time, walking out and away from the hut as he did so. And his sheep followed him.

With odd clarity, Chalky recalled something he had heard somewhere, from the Bible, he thought, that someone, sometime had taught him.

"He goeth before them, and his sheep follow him, for they know his voice. . . ."

It was symbolic, somehow, of these peasant people. Other men used trumpets to sound the charge, to excite men as they signaled them into concerted action, or to sound the retreat, or to sob out a heart-cry over the untimely dead. But these people used them — in the midst of war, of murderous chaos, they sounded them — to call patient and trusting sheep to feed on lush mountain pastures. It was simple and affecting, a vision of life as perhaps it was meant to be.

Chalky and the driver stayed for an hour's sleep and a meal. From time to time, Chalky was vaguely aware of a trumpet sounding from a distance. Once or twice he awoke, and looked at the woman, who smiled serenely. But later, as they were finishing their meal, the calls sounded more sharply, and she stood and moved unhurriedly to the door.

"Allez," she said quietly. *"Le Boche approchent."*

They thanked her, and Chalky shouldered his canvas bag, checked that the driver's package was still in it, (fearing that he might have dropped it during their climb), and they left the hut.

As they climbed together, the going got rougher. They had to edge across frequent scree slides, which tortured Chalky's unprotected feet. He gritted his teeth and kept at it, wishing all the time that he could lie down somewhere and soak his painful toes in cold water; but he was urged on by the knowledge that the crest of the range — the Spanish frontier

— was close. From time to time, also, the driver pointed, and Chalky saw, two or three ridges away, German patrols climbing doggedly, anxious to intercept them, or to drive them towards some manned border post where the Spanish could seize them and hand them over.

In a direct line from where they were at any given moment of that feverish scramble, the border was close, and getting closer, but there was no question of climbing straight up to it. They had to move in long zigzags, over spurs and ridges, or take the long way around the feet of overhanging bluffs. They had to climb steadily all day, till the agony seemed to spread from Chalky's bruised and bleeding feet, up his legs and into his back and his shoulders; and he was afraid to stop, lest he should find himself unable to start again.

The day died, the darkness came slowly, and he felt that there was no strength left in him, but just his will. But his will remained strong.

The darkness deepened, and the moon rose, sailed across the sky, and sank again; and at length, when Chalky's watch told him that it was almost midnight, they reached the top.

There, away to the right, the lights of Andorra blazed in the darkness.

It was, Chalky felt, just about the most beautiful sight he had yet seen; those free-blazing lights, after the oppressive darkness of Europe. He stood there enraptured, his light-starved eyes drinking in greedily that blaze, that sparkle, that effulgence, until the driver tugged at his sleeve impatiently, and he stumbled forward and began slithering in a diagonal plunge down the other side, into Spain.

They descended to a point about three hundred feet below the crest before the driver, admitting at last that it was becoming too dangerous to proceed any farther in the darkness and in their exhausted state, decided that they should sleep until daybreak. It was not a good place to stop, but their weariness dictated that here they should rest. Indeed, it was so steep that they had to wedge themselves against a tree to avoid rolling down the mountainside to certain injury and possible death.

They arose with the first light, stiff, cold and shivering.

For Chalky, the first hundred feet of downward climb was sheer agony; but the pain in his feet reached a crescendo, then seemed to deaden slightly. But he was limping badly when, still high up in the ranges, they came upon some Spanish peasants.

The driver went up to them, greeting them pleasantly, receiving a courteous greeting in return. In rapid Spanish, he asked the way to Setcases — and received blank stares.

"What is it?" Chalky wanted to knw. "Aren't we over the frontier yet?"

"Yes," the driver said. He didn't seem particularly pleased about it.

"So that's good — isn't it?" Chalky suggested.

One of the peasants said something, and pointed eastward.

"Gracias." The driver turned to Chalky. "We are not in the correct direction," he explained.

"We're in Spain, aren't we?"

"*Oui.* Is Spain OK. But my contact, the one to whom I must deliver the package you 'ave carry, is meet me at Setcases. We 'ave climb in the wrong direction. Setcases is east, about thirty kilometres as . . . as the crow flies. Is that 'ow you say?"

"What's that on foot?" Chalky wondered'

"On the feet, two days," the driver said glumly.

"Two days!" Chalky was aghast. Then, philosophically, he shrugged, "Oh, well, at least we're out of France."

"Two days — if we go back into France," the driver said uncomfortably.

"What? Aw, now, look —"

"No, *mon cher* Chalkee. I 'ave the package. This is what I 'ave come for. If I do not the business, I cannot afford to return. If I cannot return, I cannot 'elp others, like yourself."

"But —"

"Regard." The driver picked up a stone, and in the roadside dust he drew with it a wide curve.

"Is main range of Pyrénées," he said. "I 'ave tell you, the frontier follows the top of the ranges. If we walk around Spanish side, is long walk. We walk across the curve, like so, on French side, is not so far. Per'aps my contact will wait at Setcases."

Chalky looked at the crude diagram. Then he took out his

escape maps and checked it. The driver was right. He sighed, and put away his maps.

They turned, then, and climbed painfully back, up to the crest and over it, descending on a long, eastward diagonal. They trudged and scrambled and slithered on, seeing nobody; and as night overtook them once more, after an exhausting, pain-filled, nightmarish day, they climbed again to a point not too far below the crest, selected a stout tree and slept against it.

They were on their way again before it was fully daylight. At about midday they rested and ate, and refreshed themselves with water from a clear little burn which brawled down the mountain slope. The driver seemed slightly dejected, and Chalky sought for some word, some topic of conversation, that would lift him out of his morose silence. He couldn't think of anything, however, and he began to resent the driver's moodiness. It was all very well for him to get hosed off, Chalky thought. He was doing this trip for profit. He would, no doubt, be handsomely paid for his efforts. But Chalky himself was doing it for survival. He hadn't come from Pezens. He had come from Le Havre. He had come all the way across France. He had got across the frontier, into Spain — and here he was, back in France. And how long had it taken him? He made a quick calculation in his head.

"Hey!" he said suddenly.

The driver sat up, startled.

"It's all right," Chalky soothed him. "Relax. It's just — I've worked it out and — today's Sunday."

The driver looked at him sourly.

"No," Chalky said earnestly, "you don't get it. It's exactly three weeks to the day since I was shot down!"

"You are lucky to 'ave survive," the driver growled. Then his face relaxed into a wry grin. "You will get 'ome again," he said. "Very soon you will get 'ome again."

They moved on, presently climbing back to the crest of the ridge. The walking here was somewhat easier, for the way — and the frontier — ran along a long saddle; and below them they saw a road, on the Spanish side, and, a little distance downhill, a Spanish frontier post. Nearer at hand, some Spanish peasants were Sunday-strolling, and the two men went down and mingled with them, the driver conversing easily with some of them in his fluent Spanish.

Then, as the peasants came up to the guard post and its wooden barrier, the driver nudged Chalky, and they turned off the road and slipped past the post, through a patch of scrub, while the lackadaisical border guard's attention was occupied. They returned to the road downhill on the Spanish side, around a shoulder of hill which hid it from the border guard's view. And three hours later they entered the village of Setcases.

They walked through the main street of the little town, between blank, slightly dingy, whitewashed walls with closed doors and shuttered windows.

"We go to a safe house," was all that the driver would say.

No one seemed to take much notice of them, for which Chalky, limping and travel-stained, was profoundly thankful. There were five or six old women standing in twos and threes near the church, and an old man with a lined, strong face watched them silently from his bentwood chair beside a worn doorstep. The driver saluted him courteously, and Chalky, not speaking but simply imitating the gesture, did likewise. The old man lifted a hand and nodded gravely.

They walked right through the village, and out the other side. Chalky was glad when they had passed the last house, rounded a bend in the road, and were once more alone in the silent, hilly countryside with its flocks of skinny, goatlike sheep, its scrub, its stands of cork oak, and its olive groves dotting the brown hillsides. They came presently, as the day was fading, to a farm, a white-walled house with a cluster of outbuildings forming a hollow square. It stood amongst olive groves on a scrub-patched hillside.

It was clear that the family knew the driver, for they greeted him as an old friend. Chalky was introduced simply as the driver's friend. No names were exchanged. The man gave him a courteous *"Salutacion, Señor,"* and the woman a grave-eyed, rather shy smile. Thereafter, they respected his privacy without seeming stand-offish, ushering him into a small, plain room with whitewashed walls and furnished with an iron bedstead, a plain wooden table, a candle and a crucifix.

He sat on the bed, massaging his unhappy feet, while the driver, out in the kitchen, conversed with the man. Chalky heard his voice raised once, not, as far as he could tell, in anger, but in a tone which suggested acute disappointment. A moment or two later, he came into Chalky's room.

"I apologise," he said, "but I must leave you 'ere."

"What? Why?" Chalky asked.

"Our... mistake, when we cross the border, is make us late, one day. My contact, he could not wait."

"So what are you doing to do?" Chalky enquired. "Go home?"

"*Non.* No. I will 'ave to go on."

"Well, that's all right, then. I'll go with you."

"No. I do not go where is good for you to go, Chalkee."

"Well, at least I can go with you some of the way."

It was beginning to sound very much like a brush-off, and all sorts of suspicions began to rise in his mind. Maybe the driver had heard that the Spanish authorities were alerted, and was clearing off while the clearing was possible. He took out his escape maps and spread the one of northern Spain on the table, moving the candle aside.

"Look," he said, "according to this, I have to go south, through Ribas and Ripoll, to Barcelona. You have to go the same way, at least as far as Ripoll."

"Yes," the driver said doubtfully. "The trouble is, I 'ave to travel fast if I am to catch my contact. Your feet —. Well, I will see if I can borrow two bicycles. But... Setcases is small and poor. Two bicycles —. It may not be possible."

"See what you can do," Chalky implored.

The driver was back in less than an hour, wheeling one bicycle.

"Hélas," he told Chalky, "there was but one bicycle. It belongs to the priest. I am sorry."

"Well, what am I supposed to do?"

"You must stay 'ere. It is dangerous for you to walk. The Militia, the Police —. If they catch you, you will be interned in Miranda Concentration Camp. It is — not pleasant, one understands."

"If they catch me," Chalky said belligerently.

"They will catch you, my friend, without doubt. You speak no Spanish. You do not look Spanish. Without a guide, you are lost. My contact was to 'ave arrange matters — but now we 'ave missed 'im."

"That's all very well," Chalky argued, "but I can't stay here indefinitely."

"Is OK," the driver assured him. "When I am come to Barcelona —"

"But that's where I want to go!" Chalky said.

"When I am come to Barcelona," the driver repeated, "I will arrange matters. I must 'urry. Is only one bicycle." He held up his hand as Chalky opened his mouth to speak. "I will go to British Consulate in Barcelona," he promised, "and I will tell them you are 'ere. They will come and pick you up, never fear. They should be come tomorrow."

Chalky looked at him searchingly. He didn't like this, one bit.

"I will do it," the driver promised.

After a moment, Chalky nodded. "All right," he said. "If that's the way it's got to be. But tell them to shake their shirt, will you?"

"Pardon?"

"Tell them to hurry."

"I will tell them. Now I must go. You will be look after, here. These are very good people." The driver put out his hand, and Chalky shook it.

"Bonne chance, Chalkee," he said earnestly.

"Bonne chance," Chalky said. "And — thanks. I'm very grateful. I'll never forget what you've done."

"Ce n'est rien. It is nothing," the driver said, as they all said it, these gallant, great-hearted people who risked their very lives to help him. He asked without pause: "Where is the package?"

Chalky looked at him, grinned, and took the package from the canvas bag. "You and your bloody package."

The driver grinned, turned, and went out, through the kitchen, where Chalky heard him saying his *"Adios"* to the family; and a moment or two later saw him from the window, pedalling his bicycle down the farm track between the olive trees, and out onto the road, to be lost to sight behind a stand of cork oaks.

Chalky was alone again. It was not a pleasant feeling. For over a week he had been with people with whom he could converse, whose intentions towards him were kindly, and whose thoughts he could know. Now he was with strangers, separated from them by barriers of language and custom. With the French, you could be fairly sure that most of them were on your side against the Huns. With these people, in a fascist country, you had no such assurance.

As it turned out, the family fed him well, and were as kind as their inability to converse with him would allow them to be. That cheered him. He ate his meal, drank his wine and, excusing himself, retired to his room. There he did not light his candle, although it had become quite dark. He stood at the window, looking out to where he could see the twinkle of lights through the trees, the lights of Setcases. The lights reassured him, telling him as they did of a country not at war, with no fear of war's alarms. He would be all right, he reckoned. The driver was an all right chap. He would go to the British Consulate at Barcelona, and they, hearing that a British pilot had escaped from France and was awaiting help at Setcases, a mere seventy miles away, would utter glad cries and sally forth in a fast car, protected by diplomatic number plates, and rescue him. He undressed for the first time in three days, crawled into bed, and slept.

He awoke early next day, and rose. The washing arrange ments were a bit primitive, but they were adequate for a man who had stayed in some of the shearers' *whares* that he had stayed in. He cleaned himself up, shaved, dressed, packed his canvas bag, had his breakfast, put on his beret, and sat at the window, watching the road for the Consulate car.

The morning dragged on, soon it was noon, and his hostess brought him in a substantial lunch, with an exceedingly pleasant red wine. It relaxed him, and he returned to his vigil in a reasonably peaceful frame of mind. By about five o'clock, he resigned himself to the realisation that they were not coming today.

When he actually told himself that they were not coming, when he brought it out, as it were, into the open and examined it, he felt angry. It was bloody off-hand of them, and he would bloody well tell them so when they arrived tomorrow.

But dinner was hot and hearty, his feet had almost stopped hurting, he ate with the man and his wife, in the kitchen, where his host spoke to him cheerfully in Spanish and didn't seem to mind that Chalky could not give him any more than a smile in return; and his hostess smiled at him, and heaped his plate again, and they kept filling his glass with wine. So, at about ten o'clock, with a feeling of slightly benumbed wellbeing, he bid them all good night and went to bed, and the hell with the Consulate car.

Magnanimously, he held no grudges. They must've been busy. Or, maybe — of course! That was it. A seventy-mile bike ride took time. Suppose the driver had averaged... oh, perhaps ten miles an hour, since this was hilly country, where the Pyrénées ran down in leaps and bounds to the valley of the Segre River... ten miles an hour, seventy miles, seven hours. He left here at about seven o'clock last night. He would probably stop for a meal and a spot of shut-eye somewhere along the way. Say two hours — no, better be generous and say four hours... Chalky's brain grappled with figures, and tried to fight off sleep. Four hours plus seven hours plus, say, an hour to find the British Consulate in the city. What was that? Twelve hours. He should've been there at seven o'clock in the morning. They probably didn't open till eight. But, would he only take four hours' sleep? His contact, whom he was chasing, probably enjoyed a normal night's sleep. And presumably the driver knew where to find him, anyway. It wasn't as if he had to catch him on the road. Having missed him by a couple of days, it wasn't likely that he would catch him on the road. So, if the driver had taken eight hours sleep, he would've reached the Consulate at about midday, far too late for the Consulate staff to rearrange their day. But it should've given the Consul plenty of time to arrange for Chalky's rescue tomorrow morning. Tomorrow he would be here. In the Consulate car, seventy miles, average speed thirty miles per hour on these Spanish hill roads, less than two and

With the 2nd Tactical Air Force. In his shirtsleeves is S/L J.G. Pattison, who commanded 485 Sqn from September 1944 to February 1945.

Enjoying a tour, courtesy of the Harbour Police, on Copenhagen Harbour with Gp. Capt. D.J. Scott, Commander of 123 Wing, 2nd Tactical Air Force.

Twenty years later — Chalky White with his wife, Lorna, and daughter Mary.

"Still a formidable character . . ." Chalky and Lorna, with Air Commodc Al Deere and his w Joan, at the gates o the sheep station.

a half hours. They would probably set out first thing in the morning. Well, first thing after breakfast. Call it nine o'clock. They would be here by lunchtime.

With a contented sigh, Chalky allowed sleep to draw up over his head like a warm blanket.

Again, he rose early in the morning, washed and shaved himself, had breakfast and sat at the window, watching the road. He indulged himself in hoping that maybe the Consulate car would leave Barcelona early in the morning after all, and would be here by ten o'clock, perhaps.

But ten o'clock came, and half-past ten, and eleven o'clock, and twelve o'clock. He ate his midday meal and again returned to his post by the window. And at three forty-five, as hope was fading, he saw a cloud of dust on the road far down the valley.

He stood up, adjusted his beret with some care, made sure his wings and flashes were handy in his pocket in case the Consulate people should demand to see them, and again stood at the window, his canvas bag on his shoulder, waiting.

The dust could now be seen, a fast-dissipating, reddish cloud filtering through the oak wood. The car appeared — only, it wasn't just a car. It was a military car, flying a small Spanish flag; and it was followed by a large military truck.

He was aware, suddenly, that his hostess was standing just behind him. She said something in which he picked up the words *"Milicia"* and *"Expadriads"* and *"refugiado,"* and her tone was one of sympathetic concern . . . .

10.

Chalky stood for a moment, shocked into immobility. Then he turned swiftly, snatched up his overcoat from the bed, and took a step towards the door.

"Espera!" the woman said. She put out her hands and seized his arm. He made to shake her off, but she pointed out the window.

"No aqui!" she said.

He looked again and saw that the car and the truck had gone past, and were heading into Setcases. He looked at her, eyebrows raised, questioning.

"Refugiados," she said, slowly and distinctly, as if trying to impress something on a backward child, speaking a sort of pidgin Spanish as he might, in her place, have spoken a sort of pidgin English, in an attempt to make her understand.

"Refugiados," she said again. *"No aqui. Setcases. No aqui."* She looked into his face earnestly and, as she began to feel that he had understood, she slackened her grip on his arm, then released him, and relaxed.

They stood at the window, looking towards Setcases. They could not see anything, but faintly they heard shouted orders; and then, soon afterwards, the car and the truck went past again, down the road; and Chalky saw distinctly, as it disappeared from view, armed guards sitting at the tailboard, and crowded, white faces in the shadowed interior of the truck.

They turned and found that the farmer had come into the room. He nodded towards the road and said something about

"Milicia" and *"Puerco!"* He spat very accurately past them, out through the open window. Then he said something else about *"Idiota"* and *"imbecilidad,"* and made a gesture which Chalky had found to be international, unmistakable and rude; and the farmer laughed, and his wife laughed, and Chalky laughed, and they all had a glass of wine.

But it had shaken Chalky. As near as he could make out, the Militia had got wind of some refugees hiding in Setcases, and had swooped on them. Probably they were Jewish civilians from France. It had seemed to Chalky that practically every farm in the South of France had been hiding Jews, and smugglers had been getting them in parties across the border. He had heard of it at the farm near Arfons. His host and hostess now made rude gestures and laughed and declared the Militia to be pigs and idiots and imbeciles, but Chalky would have been prepared to bet that the arrival of the car and truck at Setcases had shocked them both. And that suggested that it was entirely possible that they would get to hear of his presence, also, and might swoop with brutal speed upon this place. He determined, therefore, to leave.

If the Consulate had been told about him, he felt, they would have come for him by now. Obviously, for whatever reason, the driver hadn't told them. The driver himself might've been picked up, for that matter — and Chalky had no reason to believe that Franco's bullyboys were any more gentle in their interrogation methods than Himmler's animals. All the more reason, he felt, for clearing out as soon as possible. Anyway, the cold, hard fact was that if the Consulate wouldn't come to him, he would have to go, like Mahomet to the mountain, to the Consulate.

He didn't know how to explain to the farm people, but in the event it proved to be easy enough. He simply came to breakfast the next morning with his canvas bag slung from his shoulder, and his beret in his hand.

"I'm off to Barcelona," he said.

"Ah," the man said, nodding wisely. *"Barcelona, si."*

"Ah," his wife said. *"Si, Barcelona."*

When he had eaten, he simply stood up, shook their hands, and said *"Gracias, sẽnor,"* the way the Mexicans did in Western movies. He shook the woman's hand warmly. *"Gracias, señora,"* he said.

The man shook his head and mumbled something that sounded like "De nada," which Chalky guessed was the Spanish version of the now familiar and humble disclaimer, "It is nothing."

He walked out to the road and down past the oak plantation. Once on the road he remembered, with something of a slight nervous tingle, the car and the truck of the day before. But the country air was still, and he was sure that he would hear the approach of a vehicle, or see its dust, in plenty of time to take cover. There was plenty of scrub about, and the olive groves and stands of tall trees, and he figured he would have no trouble getting out of sight.

Having settled on this plan of action, having dealt with the contingencies, he felt easier in his mind. It was a good day for walking, also, being overcast and cool, and he felt that he might try for a little more speed. There were, he noticed, kilometre stones along the roadside, and he began to run. He ran at a steady jog-trot for a kilometre, then walked for a kilometre, then ran again, then walked again, kilometre by kilometre. In *espadrilles* it was not comfortable, rather less so than trying to run in beach sandals, but he kept it up. He was quickly puffed, but soon got his second wind; and a painful stitch that plagued him over the first two kilometres disappeared. If it hadn't, he would still have kept up the pattern. He was so close to success that there was a sort of compulsion to run, to get over the last danger as quickly as possible.

The countryside seemed quite empty. There were no vehicles on the road, though at the top of every rise he scanned the horizon ahead for tell-tale dust clouds. He looked in every direction, except back along the way he had come. Between him and the Spanish frontier was only Setcases, as far as he knew, and there were no police or Militia establishments there. So it came as a surprise when a vehicle did come up on him from behind.

Surprise, but not alarm. It was, his ears told him, before it had even come in sight, a horse-drawn vehicle. When it did come around the bend in the road, it proved to be a boy in a dog-cart. As it approached, Chalky moved into the centre of the road and held up his hand. The boy reined up and looked at him apprehensively, without speaking.

"RAF." Chalky essayed a winning smile. The boy, not speaking, never taking his eyes from Chalky, gathered up the reins and raised his hands as though to start the pony moving again.

"Anglais," Chalky said, feeling vaguely that any sort of foreign language would have a better chance of being understood then English. He mimed making a descent by parachute. The boy stared at him for a moment longer, and raised his hands once more to flap the reins.

"I'm RAF," Chalky said quickly. He dived his hands into his pockets and produced his wings. The boy glanced at them, looked ahead again, flapped the reins and clicked his tongue at the pony, which started forward. Desperately Chalky reached out and laid a hand on the pony's bridle. It didn't stop, but Chalky held on and walked backwards with it, looking up at the boy.

"It's all right," he said earnestly. "Look, I just want a ride — a lift —"

The boy suddenly seized the whip from its socket beside the seat and lashed out at Chalky.

"Apartarse!" he shrilled.

Chalky snatched his hand away from the pony's bridle and held it up protectively before his face. The lash stung his cheek and rasped painfully across his wrist, drawing blood. He leaped back as the pony started forward, the boy whipping it into a canter. The dog-cart careered down the slope and around a bend. Chalky stood there, rubbing his cheek, watching the dust drift across the hillside.

And at that moment, it began to rain.

This was, if anything, a downpour worse than that one in the Normandy wood. It bucketed down until, within minutes, the road flowed like a river, the clay of the roadside banks melted, and it was easy to imagine that the olive trees were flattening beneath its weight.

He ran down the road, the mud grasping at his espadrilles, trying to tear them from his feet, until he came to another cork oak plantation, into which he dived. There was no shelter there at all. The rain lanced straight down through the foliage, drumming and splashing on the sodden ground. But at least, this time, he had an overcoat. He stood there morosely, hands in pockets, waiting for the rain to pass, wondering whether it would cease before his overcoat became saturated and the water began to soak through his suit. In that hour his spirits plunged somewhat.

But then he reminded himself that this was only the second shower of rain that he had had to contend with in the entire journey. That, when you came to think about it, was an amazing bit of luck. It was autumn — early autumn, but autumn just the same — and in three weeks it had rained only twice.

That made him feel a little better, but not much. There was a straightdown, unrelenting, almost crushing quality about this rain which dampened the spirits quite as much as it soaked the clothing. If there had been a wind, a good Southland sou'wester which slanted rain and drove it across paddocks in moving curtains, it wouldn't have been so bad. It would have been moving. But there was no wind at all, and no cloud movement that you could see, and it looked as though it could easily go on forever — for forty days and forty nights, Chalky thought, like Noah's downpour. "Here I am," he told himself grumpily, "like Noah — and no bloody ark!"

And it rained, and it rained, and it rained. His overcoat became heavy on him, and his beret became saturated, so that his hair under it became wet, and dribbled water down beneath the beret's edge in behind-the-ears trickles which found their way past his collar, which itself became clammy and cold.

The rain stopped at last, and he stepped out from the oak wood and back onto the road, walking over the roadside banks at first to avoid the sticky mud, until the wet grass soaked his trouser legs to the knees. Then he walked on the road again.

A rift appeared in the clouds, and broadened, and, after an hour or so, the clouds dispersed, and the sun came out. Walking, he felt his clothes drying, or at least warming, upon him. He took off his sodden beret and let the light breeze of his passing blow through his hair. He had resumed his pattern of jog-a-kilometre, walk-a-kilometre, but the going was heavy, what with the mired road surface snatching at his *espadrilles*, and the weight of his waterlogged overcoat, which he had rolled and slung across his canvas bag.

Night came, and found Chalky on a slightly improved surface. The road was running along the floor of a valley between a gully-riven, lofty peak which his map identified as Santa Caballera, and a range called the Cordillera de Santigosa. A river kept company with the road, the Rio Ter, and a narrow gauge railway sidled along a steepish slope on his left, above the road. Ahead, the lights of a village, San Juan de las Abadesas, twinkled. A dog barked, perhaps a quarter of a mile away.

Chalky decided against entering the village. According to the map that is all it was, a village, indicated by a tiny circle of exactly the same size as that marking Setcases. San Juan de las Abadesas might or might not be the same size. It could be a small town, with a police post or a Militia barracks. So he thought he wouldn't risk it, but would go down to the river, find a reasonably concealed bivouac, have some food and snatch a few hours' sleep.

He did not sleep very much, as it happened. He was cold, and his overcoat was so wet that he figured that to wrap it around himself would only make matters worse. He dared not light a fire. So he sat there, chillingly caressed by the cold vapours which moved on him across the black, glinting water; and he shivered, and occasionally got to his feet and indulged in violent calisthenics to get his circulation going. Then, briefly, slightly warm again, and uncomfortably puffed, he would sit down and nibble a piece of cheese or a hard-boiled egg or a bite of spicy sausage, and listen to the swish and clatter of the brawling river.

There is no place quite so lonesome as a riverbed, at night. The fields of the open country are empty, but the riverside is a place of plaintive sounds — the lowing of a cow or the bray of an ass, miles away, carrying mournfully over the water, as if carried downstream with the flotsam on the heedless current; the water itself, chattering, coming so close at times to the sound of human speech, underscoring the doleful fact that you are alone.

At the first sign of dawn, Chalky arose, put on his overcoat, (wet and clammy though it was), and climbed back up to the road, and from the road to the railway. He felt that the railway line would probably skirt the town, and that the railway station would be unlikely to be manned at that hour. He was right. He passed San Juan de las Abadesas and, a kilometre or so farther on, returned to the road.

At about midday, he came to Ripoll.

Ripoll was bigger than Setcases or San Juan, though how much bigger it was difficult to tell, from Chalky's point of view. It seemed to be a township rather than a village — a Lumsden rather than a Mossburn or a Dipton. And there were police in it, he knew, because even as he approached it he could see a couple of them conversing in the middle of the main street.

He kept walking towards it because, although the policemen were not even looking in his direction, they might if he started hesitating and looking furtive, or rabbiting off into the brown countryside.

Ripoll was situated on the north bank of the River Ter, almost encircled by a loop in the river, so that the way to it crossed over a stone bridge. It might be possible, Chalky thought, to find a ford downstream or upstream of the place; but Ripoll lay in a valley, and the stream, for as far as he could see, was deep and fierce, bounding down from the high country, bashing its way out from the hills, confined between rocky banks. He would probably have to go a considerable distance out of his way before he found a crossing place.

Feeling that he needed time to think this out, and tempted by the clear water, he sat down on the parapet of the bridge abutment, took off his *espadrilles* and bathed his painful feet in the water.

It was a blissful sensation, and he rather lost himself in the enjoyment of it, and did not, for the time being, give his problem serious consideration, beyond formulating a vague idea — it was too nebulous to be described as a plan — that he might hock his watch and buy a train ticket from Ripoll to Barcelona. He was sick of walking. He kept trying to turn his mind to this idea, to figure out the practical details, to plan a response to all likely contingencies; but the cooling of his bruised and lacerated feet, the easing of his anguished toes, wooed him to daydreaming.

He was shaken out of his woolgathering by a voice behind him, which asked, abruptly, *"Français?"*

Chalky looked around. A Spaniard stood there, a civilian, looking at him expressionlessly, his eyes dark and hard to read in his swarthy, saturnine, unshaven face. Because he was obviously neither a soldier nor a policeman, Chalky took a chance.

"Non." he said. *"Anglais. RAF."* With his hands he mimed coming down by parachute. The Spaniard looked at him for a moment or two more, then nodded and turned away, back across the bridge, into town.

That worried Chalky, yet something prevented him from getting up and hurrying away. He did put on his *espadrilles,* and watched the road on the other side of the bridge, where it entered the town. The man, he thought, had shown no signs of hostility or alarm. He could easily have stood right where he was and yelled for the police, and they would have heard him clear to the other end of the main street. But he hadn't.

Very soon he returned. He walked straight up to Chalky and handed him a packet of cigarettes, wordlessly. Then he moved away to a point on the roadside about a hundred yards from where Chalky sat, and watched him with a patient, unwavering stare. Chalky, more as a gesture of appreciation than because he wanted one, took out and lit a cigarette, made a gesture with it towards the Spaniard, and began to smoke it with ostentatious enjoyment.

He had almost finished his cigarette when a horse-drawn cart turned out of a side road, and headed for the bridge. It was still some distance off when Chalky recognised it for what it was — the Ripoll night-cart. Its function became more and more apparent as it came closer. The driver slowed the cart as it came near to Chalky, and signed to him to come aboard, to get, in fact, right into the tank with its hinged lid, which formed the body of the cart.

Chalky got in. He paused in the act of climbing in and gave the cigarette donor an ironic salute, which was returned, as far as he could tell, in a like spirit. Then he settled himself into the unspeakable tank, (which had been hastily hosed down, presumably for the occasion), crouching down beneath the lid, trying to hold his overcoat and his bag and his trouser cuffs off the awful floor, retaining his balance as the cart lurched over the bridge by pressing his reluctant fingertips against the bottom. The stench was indescribably vile, his stomach heaved, and he retched repeatedly; but he was getting through the town, and he was reasonably confident that no Spanish policeman would be taking the trouble to look inside this ghastly tank.

The ride seemed endless, though in reality it could have been very little more than three hundred yards. Around a bend in the road, out of sight of Ripoll, the cart stopped, and the driver, somewhat curtly, ordered Chalky out of it. Chalky had the odd impression that the fellow, hearing him gag and retch, had felt insulted.

"Thanks very much," he said. *"Gracias, señor."* The driver, not troubling to say anything in reply, but compelled by innate Spanish politeness to acknowledge Chalky's thanks with a nod, drove off and disappeared down another side road. Chalky was, once again, alone.

The road was paved, and there was more traffic on it. He tried, a number of times, to thumb a ride, though it was a bit nerve-wracking, he found, to turn and face the vehicles which were coming up from behind. There was always a possibility that he might find himself looking at a police car or a military vehicle.

But at last, after a long day, late in the afternoon, a lorry did stop. There were two men in the cab, and the one in the passenger's seat leaned out and beckoned to him. There was a sort of pad on the side of the cab, alongside the driver, exposed and dusty, and he climbed onto it and sat there gratefully as they started off down the road.

The driver, leaning towards him, eyes definitely not on the road, asked Chalky a question, and Chalky guessed that he was being asked his destination.

"Barcelona," he yelled over the engine's clatter.

The driver's mate looked at him oddly, leaned across in front of the driver, and asked: *"Français?"*

"Non. Anglais," Chalky told him. "RAF." He produced his wings.

The two men appeared to take it very calmly. They just nodded, looked briefly at each other, and kept on driving.

After a few minutes, Chalky asked, "Where are you going?"

The driver's mate, a cheerful character with a Zapata moustache and shoe-button eyes, smiled a wide, white smile.

"Si," he said.

Chalky groped for a word, some phrase that he had heard spoken in French. Some way of asking his question so that these men might understand.

"A Barcelona?" he asked, pointing at the driver, the truck, the road and himself.

"Ah!" the driver exclaimed, as if light had just dawned. "No," he said. His mate said, "No."

The driver opened and shut his mouth once or twice, nodding his head, as though trying to force out words which would not come.

"Ees tak' to — to un hombre —"

"A man?" Chalky prompted.

"Si! Si, a — man. Ees OK. 'Ave no fear, Señor RAF. *Nous te viendrons en aide."*

"Aid?" Chalky queried hopefully.

"*Si.* Ees 'elp. He weel 'elp." He looked at Chalky and smiled happily. *"Inglése OK. Franco ees puerco."* He spat through the window, and Chalky felt the spray. His mate nodded enthusiastically. "Ees peeg, Franco. *Inglése OK,"* he said, and they all laughed. The driver took both hands off the wheel, leaned out and seized Chalky's hand. He grabbed the wheel again as the lorry lurched and wandered, and his mate leaned across in front of him and shook Chalky's hand. Then they shook each other's hands, the driver and his mate, laughing. Abruptly, the driver lapsed into a morose silence, and his mate became silent and taciturn, though he occasionally glanced sidelong at Chalky and grinned. Chalky sat back and hoped that they were as sympathetic as they claimed, and would not deliver him to the police.

They turned off the main road at last. Chalky, not knowing how to ask where they were going, tried to draw some warrantable conclusion, some reassurance, from this change of direction. The road, he decided, was definitely a second-class road, a country road. It could be a short-cut to somewhere, but he reckoned that it was not, itself, leading to any major centre.

Then the driver spoke again.

"Ees go to boss," he said. "Boss ees *suizo*." The last word sounded like "swee-tho," and Chalky did not recognise it. But at least they were going to see the driver's boss; and since the driver thought that Franco was a pig, it was hardly likely that he would be working for someone with Fascist sympathies. Anyway, he could only wait and see. He wished, not for the first time since leaving Setcasas, that he had his pistol; but the driver had taken it with him when he left Chalky at the farm.

Presently, the truck turned off the road and rattled and swayed up a winding drive around the shoulder of a hill. Ahead, there came into view a long, white house with a red tile roof, a picturesque, single-storeyed place set on a shelf on the hillside, with olive groves stretching away from it, and gardens and green lawns around it, and flowers in carved wooden window boxes across its facade. They drove right up to it, around a circular carriageway, stopping at the front steps.

The man who came down to meet them was startlingly blonde, with a ruddy, open face and blue eyes.

"Ees boss," the driver said. He swung down from the cab and walked around to meet his employer. There was a brief exchange of rapid Spanish, during which the driver's mate told Chalky: "Ees boss. Ees OK." Then the blonde man came around to Chalky's side, and Chalky jumped down to meet him.

"Come along in," the man said. "I expect you could do with a drink."

It was the sweetest sound Chalky had ever heard. The English was in the accents of Oxford. The invitation was casually friendly, English-friendly.

"I sure could," he responded. He put out his hand to the driver, who shook it, and he shook the mate's hand, also. *"Gracias,"* he said. *"Mucho gracias."* He didn't know whether it was correct Spanish, but he thought it was what they said in the movies; and, anyway, they understood.

"Ees nothing," the driver said. He got back into his seat and drove off.

Chalky turned to his new host.

"My name is White, Les White, but I'm used to Chalky."

"Come in, Chalky."

As they walked up the steps, Chalky remarked that it was great to hear an English voice again.

"Thank you," the man said. "Actually, I'm Swiss."

They walked into a large, airy room with landscape windows which looked out across gardens and olive groves to scrub-patched hills and distant woods. The man stepped behind a well-equipped bar and busied himself with glasses.

"Scotch?"

"Thanks," Chalky said gratefully. Diffidently he asked, "You wouldn't have a beer about the place, would you?"

"You'd prefer a beer? By all means, Chalky. How does a long Carlsberg sound?"

"Bang on," Chalky said. "I'd still like the Scotch," he added.

"Both?"

"Is that all right?" Chalky asked anxiously.

"Perfectly, old man. Anything you want."

"It's just that I've got a throat like a lime kiln, and I've had a tough day," Chalky explained. "Beer for the thirst. Scotch to relax me."

"Of course. You're most welcome."

He opened bottles and filled glasses.

"Sit down," he invited.

Chalky looked down at himself. On the road he had seen himself as reasonably well turned-out. Not immaculate, perhaps, but definitely not vagabondish. Now, however, in the spotless, neat luxury of this room, he felt filthy. And to make matters worse, at that moment the man's wife entered the room, and was introduced to Chalky simply as "My wife." They were careful — and, Chalky guessed, wise — not to exchange names. What they were doing was dangerous. This was still a Fascist country, friendly to the Axis.

The lady was cool and fresh, fair like her husband, and delicately perfumed.

"Please sit down," she pleaded. Her English was slightly, attractively accented.

"I — I'm not too clean," Chalky said.

"Don't worry about it, old chap," the man said easily. "Make yourself comfortable. I imagine it's been a long trip."

Chalky still demurred. "I've been in — the odd place that —" he stammered, looking at the lady. The man grinned.

"It's noticeable," he said frankly. "It doesn't matter. Look, if it worries you, sit here at the bar. But for goodness sake, get off your feet. You look as if a good breeze would knock you down, man."

"I'm a bit bushed," Chalky admitted.

"Of course. Well, look, let's deal with the drinks, and then you can have a good, hot bath."

Chalky luxuriated in hot water and soapsuds for nearly an hour, after which he enjoyed a couple of hours' sleep. A servant took his clothes, and returned them miraculously laundered, brushed and aired, when he awoke.

He dined with the friendly couple. The Swiss turned out to be a millionaire who had extensive business interests in Spain. The meal was excellent, lavish with wine, and Chalky told them something of his journey through France; they asked him about his home, and seemed genuinely interested in his account of farming, and his tales of shearing in outback Australia.

It turned out, also, that they were friends of the British Vice-Consul in Barcelona.

"However," his host said, "it wouldn't be wise, I think, for me to take you to him. I think it would be better if I were to go in and tell him you're here, and let him come and fetch you. I mean, they can stop my car any time they like, and then we'd both be in trouble. But his car has diplomatic immunity, and you'd be a whole lot safer."

"Suits me," Chalky said. "I'm in your hands, sir. I'm grateful for your help."

That same night, the Swiss drove into Barcelona; the next day a car arrived, and they sent Chalky off with expressions of goodwill, with money, a good supply of cigarettes, and a tiny Spanish-English dictionary.

Chalky enjoyed the ride. The car carried a small Union Jack, and although the driver was anything but talkative, it was pleasant just to sit back and be saluted by Spanish soldiers, and waved through by Spanish policemen. He was, above all, on his way home, and he felt warmly benevolent towards the whole world — even this taciturn Consulate driver.

His reception at the Consulate was, therefore, like a bucket of cold water in the face.

He was ushered — almost marched — into a small room containing a bed, a table and two chairs. Its window, he noticed, was barred, and when his escort left him, he heard the key being turned in the lock. He was kept waiting for nearly an hour before a Consular official came in.

Chalky stood up.

"Sit," the man said brusquely.

Chalky sat.

"Name?"

"White, L.S.M."

"Full name, full name!"

"White, Leslie Samuel McQueen."

"Rank?"

"Flight Sergeant."

"Number?"

"NZ413919."

"Y-e-s," the man said doubtfully. "Squadron?"

"Four-Eight-Five," Chalky responded.

"Are you aware," the man drawled, writing something on a paper before him, "that you are authorised to give only your number, name and rank?"

"To the enemy, yes," Chalky said.

"Y-e-s. What were you flying when you were shot down?"

"A — Spitfire," Chalky said. He had been about to say, "An aeroplane," because he didn't care for this character's manner, but he didn't feel it would be wise to antagonise him.

"Aren't you sure?" the man asked.

"Of course."

"Is that all? A Spitfire?"

"That's all," Chalky said, nettled. "You can only fly one at a time."

"Don't get clever with me, Flight Sergeant," the official snapped. "You know perfectly well what I mean."

"Spitfire 9b," Chalky told him. "If that means anything to you," he added.

The man opened his mouth, shut it again, and paused. He produced a packet of Gold Flake cigarettes which, Chalky could see, was clearly stamped "H.M. Forces." He pushed it across the table. Smiling a vinegary smile, he said, "Look, we're getting off on the wrong foot. I'm just doing my job, you know."

Chalky took a cigarette from the packet and stowed the pack in his pocket.

"Those are my cigarettes," the man said. Chalky took the pack from his pocket, looked at it, and said: "Are you in His Majesty's Forces?"

"No," the man said, "But —"

"Well, I am," Chalky said. "These cigarettes were clearly intended for me." He replaced the pack in his pocket, lit the cigarette that canted up insolently between his lips, inhaled luxuriously, and sat back, looking at his interrogator.

"Suppose," the man said, "that I were to tell you that Four-Eight-Five Squadron doesn't fly 9bs?"

"They did when I was there," Chalky said.

"Ah, yes. When you were there. How long ago was that?"

"I make it three weeks and four days ago," Chalky said.

"And on what date were you shot down?"

"The twenty-second of August," Chalky said, adding as if to make something clear to a not-very-bright child, "nineteen-forty-three."

The man looked at him sharply.

"Three and a half weeks ago," he said. "You must've passed through France amazingly quickly. Two or three days, in fact."

"Three weeks exactly it took me to get to the Spanish frontier," Chalky said.

"Ah. Then it's three and a half weeks since you escaped.

When were you shot down, then?"

Chalky sighed. "On the twenty-second of August," he said. "You just wrote it down."

The man sat back and looked at Chalky, frowning.

"Are you saying that you are not an escaper, but an evader?"

The difference, in Chalky's opinion, was almost hair-splitting.

"I got away from the Huns," he said. "What's the difference?"

"An escaper," the man told him, "is one who's been captured and been in enemy custody. An evader is one whom they've never caught."

"Then I'm an escaper," Chalky told him.

"Are you sure?"

"Bloody hell!" Chalky exploded. "Wouldn't I be? I know what happened to me."

"You say," the man persisted, "that you were shot down on the twenty-second of August. That's three and a half weeks ago. You say you took three and a half weeks to get across France and down here, to Barcelona. Yet you also maintain that you were a prisoner of the Germans. Haven't you got your story a bit fouled up, my lad?"

"No," Chalky said.

"Then there's something very strange about its arithmetic."

"I don't get you," Chalky said.

This time it was the man who sighed.

"Tell me," he said with martyr-like resignation, "for how long were you a prisoner?"

"About three quarters of an hour," Chalky said.

"Oh."

"Anything else you want to know?" Chalky asked accommodatingly.

"Where were you shot down?"

"Near Le Havre."

"I see. And what happened?"

Chalky told him. As he did during his interrogation by the driver, he omitted crucial place-names, and such names as he knew of the people who had helped him. In the case of the driver, he had done it because he knew that he could be being tricked by the Gestapo or the Vichy police; or, if his interrogators were genuine, they could be arrested at some time, and the names wrung out of them by torture. In the present case, he was cautious because he was beginning to wonder about the intelligence, and therefore the discretion, of this Consulate official. It was not a fair assessment, he now acknowledges, but the habit of caution had become deeply ingrained.

As he ended his story, it seemed to him that he ought to clear up the part concerning the driver leaving him at Setcases.

"He had to catch his contact," he explained. "He promised he would come and tell you where I was. I waited for you for a couple of days, but when you didn't show up, I figured that he hadn't managed to see you."

"Oh, he saw us," the official said.

"What? Then why the hell didn't you come?" Chalky asked hotly.

The official regarded him with a cold and fishy-eyed stare.

"Do you expect us to go swanning off on the word of every doubtful-looking character who comes in? The man could've been a Franco agent-provocateur, trying to get us to compromise ourselves. Or a Nazi sympathiser, trying to get us to accept a German as English."

Then, dismissing that episode altogether, he returned to the attack.

"What you're saying is," he said, "that you came all the way across Occupied and Vichy France by yourself. You're trying to make me believe that you sought out assistance on your own. You walked on your own. You bought train tickets, food, on your own. The only time you received assistance from the Underground was when you crossed into Spain. Is that right?'"

"That's right," Chalky said, glad that the official had got it right at long last.

"You speak fluent French, of course," the man said.

"No," Chalky said. "No French, except a word or two I picked up on the way."

"Or German?"

"Not a word."

"Or Spanish?"

"No."

"Then your story doesn't sound very probable, does it." He glared at Chalky, then sat back and bounced his papers together.

"You will be kept here, for the time being," he said. "Frankly, Flight Sergeant Leslie Samuel McQueen White, I don't believe you. An educated man, maybe. A man familiar with Europe, it might just be possible. Even then, the odds against such an escape must be astronomical. Well, we shall see. I shall cause — certain inquiries to be made. Meanwhile, I must act on the assumption that you are a spy. You will remain here, for the time being, under surveillance."

11.

Chalky was stunned.

He refused to show his feelings, however, and simply shrugged.

"Want some names of my squadron mates?" he suggested.

"I shall talk with you again," was all the official would say.

"One thing —" Chalky said.

"What's that?"

"Can you get me a pair of size eleven shoes?" Chalky asked.

The answer he received was a bleak stare. Then the man walked out of the room, locking the door behind him.

Chalky sat there for a time. This, he thought, was unbelievable! The man said he thought he was a spy! How could he be a spy? And a spy for whom? He didn't speak French, Spanish or German. He'd told the man that. But then, of course, the man didn't believe him.

The official came back after an hour or two, no more friendly than before.

"You've checked up on me?" Chalky asked.

"Hardly."

"But you said you were going to make certain inquiries."

"It takes time," the man said. "Has to be done through the diplomatic pouch — as you probably know quite well."

"There's radio," Chalky said.

"Codes can be broken," the official replied.

He sat down, and once more they faced each other across the table.

"Name?" the offical asked.
"White, Leslie Samuel McQueen."
"Home address?"
"Strathway, Gore, Conical Hill R.D., Otago, New Zealand."
"Ah, yes. A New Zealander. You don't look much like a New Zealander, to me."
"What does a New Zealander look like?" Chalky wondered.
"English," the official said shortly, "or Maori."
"Come to that," Chalky said, "you don't look all that English to me."
"Don't be impertinent, Flight Sergeant."
"Anyway," Chalky said, "why should I look English? I'm of Scottish, Irish and Maori descent, with a little bit of Jewish thrown in. What could be less English than that?"
"Next-of-kin?" the official asked coldly.
"Mrs J.I. White."
"Same address?"
"Yes."
"Wife?"
"Mother," Chalky said.
"Date of birth?"
"May 24th, 1917."
"Place of birth?"
"East Gore, Southland."
"All right," the official said, more to himself than to Chalky. He wrote for a moment, then looked at Chalky again.
"What is Strathway? I mean, is it a village? A farm? A geographical locality?"
"A farm," Chalky said.
"How big?"
"Three hundred acres," Chalky said. "Sheep, and a few head of Aberdeen Angus cattle."
"Gore?"
"The nearest town."
"I see. And Conical Hill is a rural delivery zone, I take it?"
"That's right."
"Where is Southland?"
"Bottom end of the South Island," Chalky told him.

"Really? According to my atlas, that's Otago," the man said. He sounded triumphant, as though he had found at last a fatal flaw in Chalky's story.

"Well, your atlas is wrong," Chalky said flatly. "The boundary starts just north of Milford Sound, runs down the south shore of Lake Wakatipu, and through the Pukerau hills to Chasland's Mistake on the east coast. Does that answer your question?"

"More than adequately," the official said. "I think you've been well taught."

"Bloody hell, I live there!" Chalky exclaimed. "I've ridden horseback all over that district."

"Y-e-s," the man said sceptically. "Squadron?"

"Four-Eight-Five, flying Spit Nines."

On the first interrogation you said Spitfire 9bs," the official said.

"Look," Chalky roared, "I've told you who and what I am. I've had a bloody long walk. I'm tired, mate. I'm sick of being treated like a bloody spy. I'm sick of this bloody room. I'm sick of you. I want to get back to my squadron — and I'm telling you, if the bloody Huns couldn't stop me, I'm damned sure you can't. Now, are you going to help me, or not? Because, if not, I'll find some other way of getting back, and the hell with you!"

The man looked at him coldly.

"It won't help you to take that attitude," he said. "As far as we're concerned, your whole story is suspicious in the extreme. If a German agent wanted to get into Britain, this could be a reasonably easy way of doing it. You could be impersonating a captured or killed British airman. And if that's so, it explains very well why you, alone of all British escapers, did *not* seek the help of the Underground. You could much more easily and safely be taken to the frontier by Germans and brought in by Spanish agents. That's the whole, fatal weakness of your story. Nobody has ever come through France without the help of the Underground. It's highly improbable that anyone could, or would even want to try."

"Have you ever escaped through France?" Chalky demanded.

"No, of course not, but —"

"Then you don't know anything about it," Chalky said. "You just haven't got a clue what you're talking about, so why don't you just shut up?"

The man reddened.

"Don't try taking that tone to me," he said. "I'm making some inquiries. The answers should be back in a day or so. Meanwhile, you'll be confined to quarters in the Consulate."

It took them the best part of a week to check with the RAF in Britain through the diplomatic pouch; and even when they had satisfied themselves of Chalky's *bona fides*, they were not exactly gracious. He acknowledges, now, that they had reason to be cautious; but it was galling, such a chilling reception after what he had been through.

One week to the day after his arrival at the Consulate, they sent him by car, cleared of all suspicion of espionage, to the British Embassy in Madrid. Delighted to be free from the Consulate, still in his French civilian suit, and still with *espadrilles* on his raw and painful feet, he lounged back in his seat like a VIP, graciously acknowledging the salutes of the Spanish soldiers and police, and enjoying the scenery.

It was good just to be able to give the scenery his full and undivided attention, to examine the landscape without having to assess its potential as a route or a hiding place. There was much to interest him, and he was especially intrigued to notice that many of the bridges they crossed on their way to the capital were pontoon structures, replacements for bridges destroyed in the Civil War.

The British Embassy officials seemed friendly enough, but Chalky found himself delivered into the care of an RAF Group Captain, whose demeanour suggested that Chalky's advent was rather a nuisance, an unwelcome disturbance in the tranquil tenor of his days. Soon after Chalky's arrival, a group of other RAF escapers arrived, men who had come through France with Underground assistance, and who, like Chalky, found the coolness of their reception disconcerting.

One manifestation of this coolness was the food. It was plentiful, but monotonous, consisting as it did of tinned M & V, (meat and vegetable mixture with rather a predominance of potato and vegetable marrow), and bully beef, which was, for the benefit of those who never had the dubious privilege of eating field rations, a very dry, very salty canned corned beef.

Chalky was convinced that the Embassy staff in general and the Group Captain in particular enjoyed rather more sumptuous provisioning, and he ventured to complain. He asked, also, if they could procure for him some shoes, size eleven.

"Size eleven," he was told by a blandly bored official, "are unlikely to be obtainable, I'm afraid." He did not even offer to shop around.

"Too bad," one of Chalky's fellow escapers commiserated.

"Too bad?" Chalky said hotly. "Too bloody right it's too bad! We'll see about this."

With the money given to him by the Swiss millionaire, he sought out an Embassy servant and persuaded him to go out into the city and buy him a pair of size eleven shoes. The man was perfectly willing.

"Hang on!" Chalky told him as he was about to go. "What about tucker?" he asked the other escapers. Together, and with the Spanish servant's recommendations, they compiled a list of foodstuffs and wines.

When the man returned, laden with his purchases, Chalky put on this new shoes, which were a very red tan, took a few experimental paces this way and that about the room, and pronounced himself profoundly satisfied.

"Now," he said to his companions, "I think it's about time I went and had a word with the Groupie."

It should be explained that there were, in those days, flying group captains — that is, group captains who were closely involved and not infrequently taking part in air operations — and non-flying group captains, usually in various staff and administrative appointments. The rank is equivalent to naval captain or army colonel. Most non-flying group captains were gentlemen, men who had, in many cases, fought in the murderous affrays between stick-and-string machines of the First World War, and who now served in positions where their experience and know-how would be of the greatest benefit; but some of them, from a mere flight sergeant's point of view, gave the impression of being majestic beings very close to divinity. You didn't speak to such group captains in the ordinary course unless they first spoke to you; and their verbal communications with the lower orders seldom expanded beyond a simple and direct question or observation, requiring at most a brief and respectful "Yes, sir," or "No, sir." For an NCO or a common erk to arrange an interview with such a group captain was not merely unheard of. The very idea amounted almost to blasphemy. It was, for all practical purposes, outside of the bounds of possibility.

Chalky's companions, therefore, were pardonably sceptical, and smiled mockingly when he made his announcement.

But then, Chalky had not actually applied for an interview. Furthermore, he had no intention of making such an application. His arrangements were already made to his own satisfaction, and he felt no need of permission or third-person approval.

As he made his way through the consequential corridors of His Britannic Majesty's Embassy in Madrid, his bright red shoes squeaking on the long expanses of parqueted floor, his new scarlet shirt, (purchased for him by the Embassy servant to replace the rags of his RAF issue shirt), adding to the glow of rosewood and mahogany doors and shaming the pallid colouring of the superb ornamental plasterwork, all of his frustration, all of his sense of injustice and outrage, was coming to the boil. He came at last to a door with the Group Captain's name on it, flung it open without ceremony, slammed it behind him and advanced into the room, his dander travelling before him almost visibly, like a bow wave. The Group Captain, startled into a frozen immobility, sat staring at him from behind a vast desk.

"I want a word with you, mate," Chalky grated.

The Group Captain did not bluster or stutter. He had an icy presence, backed by absolute faith in the inviolability of his position.

"I beg your pardon, Flight Sergeant?" he snapped.

But Chalky, who had, in his time, stood toe-to-toe, eyeball-to-eyeball with an Australian shearers' union shop steward, was not cowed.

"In our quarters," he said, "there are blokes who have just come through France. They were shot down in combat. They were taken prisoner by the Huns — who, incidentally, frequently showed 'em more respect and better treatment than we've had here — and they escaped. It's no game, you know. Those bastards are likely to shoot you. If they don't shoot you, they're likely to torture you, just to get the names of people who've helped you. We've all run that risk. We've all been wet, tired, hungry, alone. A whole lot of ordinary, decent people have put themselves and their families at risk to help us escape. But you — what've you done?"

The Group Captain might have put matters to rights there and then without loss of dignity. But he chose to bluster. He stood up.

"I will not countenance —" he began, but Chalky overrode him.

"I arrived here with bruised and bleeding feet, and no proper shoes. When I asked for shoes, what happened?"

"This is not an Air Force Station," the Group Captain said. "We have no clothing store here."

"I'll tell you what bloody happened," Chalky said. "I bought my own bloody shoes, that's what happened. And the food! Bully beef and tinned M & V! And don't hand me any malarky about no food store here. Do you live on bully beef and M & V? I'll bet!"

"I will not stand here and be subjected to this insolence, Flight Sergeant!" the Group Captain stormed, thumping the desk. Chalky, not to be outdone, thumped his side of it.

"I'll tell you what," he said. "When I get back to England, I'm going to report you. Someone's going to hear about this, and hear it loud and clear. And if the RAF isn't interested, I'll tell the Air Ministry; and if they don't do anything about it, I'll complain to Bill Jordan."

"Bill Jordan?" the Group Captain asked, curious in spite of his own fury.

"The New Zealand High Commissioner," Chalky said. "He keeps an eye on us. We're his boys, and you can bet the scrambled eggs on your hat that if the New Zealand Government gets word of the deal you've been handing us, they'll kick up at the highest level, and I reckon you'll be rooted out of your cushy job quick and lively. That's all I've got to say to you — sir."

He turned and walked out, slamming the door behind him again. He was almost shaking with anger. "If I wasn't such a disciplined bastard," he told his delighted fellow escapers, "I'd've belted him."

Little by little, he cooled down, and began to chuckle about the episode, remembering the expressions which had chased across the Group Captain's empurpled face, and the consternation with which he had discovered that here was a man who wasn't in awe of his rank and position.

But it has to be recorded that Chalky's outburst made little practical difference while he was there. They ate better because they sent out and bought better food. But the only other improvement, as far as they were concerned, was that they didn't see the Group Captain again during the ten more days that they stayed at the Embassy. Odd secretaries seemed to look at them with a new respect, Chalky felt, and once or twice he received what he believed was a knowing grin. Whether it was a grin of approval, or of anticipation at the retribution that would fall on him whenever he got home, Chalky wasn't sure. He didn't really care. It did nothing to relieve the acute boredom. The tension, the excitement, was over, and there was no activity, nothing to help them "train off".

On the 1st October, the eleventh day of their stay at the Embassy, they were told to get their gear together. Glad to be leaving, they assumed that they were on their way to Gibraltar. But they were loaded onto a truck and driven to the railway station where, to their dismay, they found themselves handed over to an escort of Spanish police. They looked at one another, and Chalky remembered the driver's warning about Miranda Concentration Camp.

"I'm not going with them," he told the others in a low voice. But the Embassy official reassured them.

"It's perfectly all right," he said. "Arrangements have been made on your behalf. You are to be taken to the frontier with Gibraltar, where you will be handed over to your own people. I'm coming with you, so just do whatever you're told without argument. He looked at Chalky with a faint grin as he said it. "You'll be free in a few hours," he promised.

And so they were — delightfully free, in British territory, where they celebrated hilariously. The RAF authorities in Gibraltar were slightly nonplussed, but understanding. The escapers' behaviour was a bit wild, not at all the kind of behaviour envisaged by the compilers of King's Regulations and Air Council Instructions, and certainly not the kind that could be safely condoned in garrison troops. But the same authorities were combat-experienced people, here on active service, and they understood, and stretched quite a few points. Gladly, but without a single reproach, they loaded their light-headed, high-spirited charges onto a Liberator bomber for the flight back to England, a somewhat piratical crew whose newly-issued Mae Wests and parachute harness hardly hid motley — and, in Chalky's case, garish — sets of civilian clothing, entirely out of place with the issue revolvers they wore in blue webbing holsters on their hips as regulation equipment for what was counted as an operational flight.

A quietness settled on Chalky and his companions once they were aboard. It was over. The great Adventure was ended. In a few hours they would set foot again on English soil. Chalky expected that they would get a bit of leave, and then be back in the war again.

It was hot in the Liberator. It sat on the edge of the tarmac apron in front of the control tower, its pilots poking about doing their pre-flight inspection of airframe and engines. Chalky, sitting by a midships window, looking out at the shimmering airfield and the waters of the bay and the crowded dockyard, began to nod. In his drowsing state, he imagined for a moment that he was on the train, travelling south from Reuilly. It became mixed up in his dreaming brain with the journey from Chateauroux to Toulouse, and the German train control was entering the carriage, and he was pretending to be asleep.

"Come on, Flight," a voice kept saying, and a hand grasped his shoulder and shook him. He snored for effect.

"Come on, Flight. Wakey-wakey," the same cheerful London voice insisted. Chalky opened his eyes.

"What's up?" he asked the RAF corporal.

"You've been off-loaded, you lot."

"What? What for?"

"Come on, Chalky," one of the other escapers said.

"VIP flight," the corporal told him.

Chalky stood up.

"When do we get away now?" he asked.

"Search me, Flight," the corporal said.

As they stepped out onto the tarmac beneath the brilliant Mediterranean sunshine, a small cavalcade of staff cars drove towards them, across the apron in front of the hangars, past the parked aircraft.

"Come on," the corporal insisted, trying to shepherd them, these inconvenient escapers in their scruffy, travel-stained mufti, out of the way, out of sight of the VIPs, whoever they were.

Looking back as the car passed by, Chalky caught a glimpse of khaki uniforms and red tabs. He stood there, he and his companions, trying to see who it was, wondering if it could be, inclined to believe that perhaps it was, the legendary Monty, or maybe even Churchill, or the King. But the VIPs got out of the other side of the car, and were promptly surrounded by officers. With the corporal trying vainly to persuade them to move on, the escapers stood and watched the flurry of saluting, and heard the brief laughter. Then khaki-clad figures were climbing into the Liberator.

All at once, Chalky felt resentful. There it was, the link with England, the last leg of the journey to England, and it was going without him. Possibly the others felt the same about it. Whatever their thoughts, whatever their reasons, they all stood there, watching the Liberator taxi out to the head of the runway. The corporal stood and watched it, too, patient, realising what it must mean to them, knowing positively that they wouldn't come until the Liberator was out of sight.

Its engines ran up, one by one; and then it began to roll forward, faster, and faster, and faster yet, rising into the air, tucking its tricycle undercart into its nose and its wings, rising up, out over the bay.

Suddenly, it seemed to stagger in the air. Grotesquely, like a walrus attempting graceful aerobatics, it rolled right over.

It seemed to be happening in slow motion. Over it went, and over; and down it came, upside down, in a perfectly smooth, long arc, and plunged into the sea....

For a long time the little group stood there, while sirens sounded and rescue launches churned out across the bay in a vain search for survivors. And at last, silent, each wrapped in his own thoughts, a slowly-moving little band of solitudes, they walked towards the hangars and the white and noisy town, and the towering Rock.

"It could've been me," Chalky kept thinking. "I could be dead." And it began to weigh down on him, that horrifying plunge into the sea; and the people at the Vice-Consulate, who thought he was a spy; and the gunfight in the moonlit potato field; and the Gestapo on the Yvetot-Paris train; and the soldiers poking into outbuildings and digging their bayonets into the manure heap in the Normandy farmyard; and the FW190s on his tail, pumping 20mm shells into his crippled Spitfire.

"I could be dead."

It numbed him. It sat on his shoulder and whispered in his ear as, eventually, he was flown back to England. It sat on all their shoulders, so that the crew which ferried them home marvelled at the glumness of men who had everything in the world to rejoice over.

It kept at him, weighed upon him, through the interrogations, the medical checkups, the ride in the Austin van in its faded camouflage colours which took him home to Biggin Hill.

The van dropped him before the door of the Sergeants' Mess, and he stood there uncertainly, unable to get used to the idea that he didn't have to search for words and signs, that he wasn't confined out of sight, that there were no officials placing strictures upon him, that from here on it was taken as a matter of course that he knew where to go and what to do.

Still as in a dream, he walked into the Sergeants' Mess, and someone at the bar glanced casually around, did a perfect double-take, and shouted: "Well, I'll be —! Look who's here! Chalky, you old sinner!"

They crowded around him, and made facetious remarks about the Station Warrant Officer wanting to put him on a fizzer for being AWOL, and holidays on the Continong, and the cut of his suit. Someone thrust a beer into his hand, one of those enormous one-pint pewter tankards, and he looked into it, and at them; and suddenly the imp on his shoulder fled, and the megrims disappeared, and the old fire flamed up in him.

"I've got better things to do," he said, "than hanging about in bloody France."

"Line! Line!" someone yelled, but nobody took it up. Looking at him, at that six-foot, broad-shouldered frame, that frank and fearless blue eye, they knew that he wasn't shooting a line. He meant every word that he said. Chalky White had better things to do than hanging about in France.

So — he came on home.

EPILOGUE

It was and is in the nature of Chalky White to shrug such things off lightly. The past is the past. You try something — and you either succeed or fail. It all comes to the same thing, in the long run. Succeed or fail, you still have to go on for as long as there's breath in your body. Each day is a new beginning. Your success or your failure alike will equip you for each new task, each new beginning.

Of course, each experience will leave some kind of mark, on you and on others.

The German guard, for example, from whom Chalky escaped. If he is still alive, is he bitter about it? Did he suffer for it? Does it still affect him? Or is it, forty-odd years later, on episode which has lost its power to hurt, and merely remains a subject for faint wonder? "Did it really happen to me?"

It affected others. These things always do — because we don't live only unto ourselves. The events of our lives don't occur in some kind of vacuum.

Chalky's mother was profoundly affected. On the morning of the twenty-fifth of August, probably about the time that Chalky was creeping into the empty stable, his mother was staring wide-eyed and white-faced at the telephone. Still holding the receiver in her hand, she heard, thin and piping, the voice of the operator at Gore, asking anxiously if she was all right; but in her mind she was still listening to his taut voice reading out the telegram:

> Regret to inform you that your son Leslie Samuel McQueen White has been reported missing on air operations on 22nd August 1943. The Prime Minister desires me to convey to you on behalf of the Government his deep sympathy with you in your anxiety. Letter following. F. Jones Minister of Defence.

The cynic may snort at the idea that the Government really felt for her one way or the other. After all, much has been written of brief, coldly worded, heartless telegrams impersonally delivered, shattering blows in cold officialese. It may be so elsewhere — but it was not true in New Zealand. Even then, the promised letter was on its way. Mr T.A. Barrow, the Air Secretary, had written:

> Dear Mr White,
>
> Further to the telegram sent to you by the Hon. the Minister of Defence concerning your son, Flight Sergeant Leslie Samuel McQueen White, I have to advise that the following information has been received from Air Ministry:
>
> Flight Sergeant White was pilot of a fighter type aircraft which took off on air operations at approximately 6pm on 22nd August, 1943 and failed to return to its base, the result, it is presumed, of enemy action. Flight Sergeant White has consequently been classified as missing.
>
> I am enclosing a copy of a memorandum on the steps being taken to trace missing air personnel in order that you may see what is being done. On behalf of the Air Board, I desire to express my deep sympathy with you in your great anxiety. You will be advised immediately any further information is received.

Enclosed was the promised memorandum, which outlined the steps taken through the International Red Cross Committee in Geneva to trace missing personnel, with assurance that as soon as anything was known, next-of-kin would be advised. It mentioned also that other sources, unspecified, were being checked. A smaller, separate notice advised that for security reasons, no announcement should be made privately to the press until after the official casualty-list notification had appeared in the papers. It said that, also for security reasons, there might be some delay before official notification was given in the casualty lists, and that this delay could range from three weeks in the case of death or wounds to six weeks in the case of missing personnel.

It promised nothing, but somehow it helped, giving her the feeling that the high-ups cared, that they were doing something about it, and that they knew what they were doing.

On twenty-second September, one calendar month after the day on which Chalky was shot down, his mother received another letter from Air Department. The intervening month had been one of struggle, fighting against the fear that he was dead, bringing to bear on the situation all of her knowledge of him, of his hardiness, his enterprise, his toughness. The news had come as a profound shock, naturally, and all the more severe because hitherto all she had known of his war was what he had written in his letters to her, thanking her for the gifts of socks and lovingly knitted pullover; letters taken up with the little matters — the cake that had arrived safely, the numbered letters which had not yet reached him. Somehow, it had built in her mind a picture of a boy doing a technical job, a fringe job, not without danger, perhaps, but not, in her mind, connected with the horrific scenes presented in newsreel films and newspaper stories. She knew — of course she knew — that he could become a casualty, (a euphemism surely invented for the comfort of mothers), but she never acknowledged to herself that she knew.

Now came the second letter, a thoughtful note, from the Air Secretary. It told her that her son had been promoted to the rank of Pilot Officer, with effect from the 21st August, the day before he had been shot down. It was cold comfort, in a way, yet it warmed her somewhat that they had taken the trouble to tell her. The letter ended:

> In conveying this news to you I trust that the knowledge that your son's fine services have been recognised by the granting of a commission will in some small way be a consolation to you in your great anxiety.

Reading it and re-reading it, she clutched at the small ray of hope it offered her, a hope which would have been no hope for anyone but an anxious mother. If they thought he was dead, they would hardly have bothered to put his promotion through. They might just know something, might possess some indication of his survival.

There was one other letter from a member of the Air Board. Air Commodore Bannerman, Air Member for Personnel, wrote to her, telling her personally what had already been told by the memorandum — that it could take some time for news of her son to get through, amplifying it to the extent of pointing out that this was inevitable due to security precautions and the exigencies of wartime communications. It ended with words of simple and honest condolence.

And when at last he reached the safety of Gibraltar, they were quick to inform her that he was safe "in neutral territory", and gave her a London address through which she could write to him, warning her that he must be addressed as Mr L.S.M. White. The waiting, the hoping, the agonised prayers were forgotten in a jubilant inflooding of thankfulness. Leslie, her son, was safe.

His friends were affected somewhat differently. When you had a friend, and he was shot down, you didn't dwell on it. It was a long war. Your personal survival depended on a modicum of luck and a heaping helping of skill. Reduced to the equation's simplest terms, the survivor in any encounter was the one whose reactions were quickest and whose skill was greatest. Sooner or later it was probably inevitable that you would run up against someone quicker, more skilful, less strained, fresher than yourself. The only variable, the only factor which remained in your favour as time went by, was luck. So you didn't stop to acknowledge the finality, or even the fact, of a friend's death. You tossed it off with some laconic observation, some piece of outrageous understatement. You never said, "He's dead." You said, "He's gone for a Burton," a phrase taken from a series of advertisements for a brand of British beer. The one thing you certainly didn't do was mope.

So the reception in the Sergeants' Mess, the casual acceptance of his survival, was typical. His return from the dead was greeted with the same laconic wisecracking, the same light humour, as his disappearance. He wasn't hurt or insulted. It was how he preferred to treat the matter himself.

One of the first things he did was to ring the Squadron Office to announce his return formally. The call was answered by a Flying Officer Gibbs.

"G'day," Chalky said in his gravelly growl. "That you, Gibbie?"

There was a longish pause. Then: "If I didn't know better," Gibbs said uncertainly, "I'd say that was Chalky White? Man, I thought you'd bought it. Where are you ringing from?"

"Berlin," Chalky told him solemnly.

His reception by the Station Commander, the great "Sailor" Malan, was typical of that irascible ace, and because it was so, it failed to dampen Chalky's spirits, and served to usher him back to normality, into the state of things-as-they-were.

"OK," Malan said matter-of-factly, "so you're back. There's only one reason why you're back, and that is that the Germans have no guts."

From anyone else, Chalky felt, he wouldn't have taken that. To anyone else he'd have suggested that they set themselves down in Normandy and have a go. But with a man like Malan, you had the feeling that he could've done exactly that, and heaven help the Hun who got in his way. So he accepted it cheerfully.

"I've been posted here," he said.

"That's right," Malan agreed. "Well, there's work to be done, White. The war's not over yet. You're down for an op. tomorrow. Now, go and get out of that appalling suit, and spruce yourself up a bit. Oh, and by the way, your promotion's through. Pilot Officer. You'll be in the Officers' Mess."

Chalky, grinning, walked out of the office, across the tarmac, heading for the Officers' Mess. A friend of his, Flight Lieutenant Lee, came towards him, making for his Spitfire, parachute slung over his shoulder.

"G'day, Chalky," he said absently, and walked on. Chalky turned, surprised at this casual reception, and was in time to see Lee stop suddenly, and stiffen like a man struck by lightning, drop his parachute and come running back to him. "Where did you spring from?" he demanded.

Reactions like that, Chalky felt, made it all doubly worthwhile. He was later to learn that his squadron commander, Squadron Leader Martin Hume, received word of his return while dining with Al Deere. His reaction was the very opposite to the satisfying shock exhibited by Lee.

"Always said he'd be back," he murmured, and went on eating.

Chalky himself quickly put the whole episode behind him. A new day, he figured. A new beginning. But matters conspired to make that a difficult thing to do.

For a start, it wasn't all that easy to get back into the swing of things. The escapers hadn't left Gibraltar empty-handed, these give-it-a-goers. It wasn't to be thought, for example, that men with such a penchant for seizing the main chance would have passed up the splendid opportunity offered by Gibraltar of obtaining all those little luxuries which severely rationed Britain could not afford. They arrived at Bristol laden with such essentials as cigarettes and grog in sufficient quantities to have started a modest supermarket. Such a quantity and assortment of wines and spirits was there that a Customs Officer, mindful of grim duty, confiscated the lot. That was a mistake. Chalky, for whom civilized and law-abiding intercourse had been a laughable half-memory for the past six fraught weeks, reacted in an exceedingly forthright, most un-British way. He lugged out his issue revolver, poked it into the Customs Officer's fair round belly and suggested with his gravelly growl that the grog and stuff be returned forthwith, which it was. He presumes that the RAF must have squared things with the disgruntled officer, because no more was heard about the incident.

Hustled off to London, the group was put up in a somewhat economy-class hotel, and taken thence to MI6 for interrogation. Chalky retains to this day his copy of the report he gave them, headed MOST SECRET and rigorously censored with scissors and Scotch Tape before even he was allowed to take it away.

He reported, at that time, the FW190s he had seen practising climbing turns over the airfield near Toulouse, and a squadron of Mustangs went over straight away and paid the airfield a visit. They destroyed most of the aircraft on the ground, which must have been rather a shock for pilots undergoing operational training on a supposedly safe airfield in the middle of supposedly neutral Vichy France.

He learned from his interrogation, incidentally, that on that day, six weeks earlier, the Squadron had been warned by the radar people of the approach of a massive formation of German fighters. It didn't, of course, make any difference. It couldn't. The Spitfire boys were there to protect the bombers, whatever the odds might be. The bomber formation was the primary factor, the main thrust. It was not for them to tangle with the Luftwaffe in the air. (For that matter, the escorting Spitfire pilots were under orders to charge any intercepting enemy head-on and punch through them. S/Ldr. Johnnie Checketts, leading the Spitfires, proceeded as planned, and presently looked around to find himself alone and lonely.) The bombers' task was to clobber the German fighter base at Beaumont le Roger. The Spitfires were there to facilitate the bombers' task. They did so. The raid was successful, with no bombers lost, and that was what really counted.

But by Chalky's arithmetic, the fighters' part in the operation was highly successful, also. The Spitfires' official score was four enemy fighters destroyed for the loss of four Spitfires. Chalky's tally said five enemy aircraft destroyed. One of the damaged Spitfires made it back to England before crash-landing. One pilot, Fraser Clark, a young pilot officer from Wanganui, was killed. "Gentleman Jack" Rae, a Flying Officer, collided in mid-air with the wreckage of a German fighter which he was shooting off the tail of another Spitfire, and crashlanded in the paddock next to Chalky's field, to be taken prisoner. Flight Lieutenant Mac Sutherland had a leg almost blown off, but parachuted to the ground safely, was taken to a hospital by the Germans, where his leg was amputated, and eventually was taken to a POW camp. And, of course, Chalky got home. He reckons the RAF won on points.

The MI6 interrogation over, Chalky was free to return to his hotel. First, however, he thought it might be a good idea to drop into the New Zealand Forces Club in Charing Cross

Road, just to see if he could spot any of his squadron mates. In an ensemble in which the Air Force blue of his jacket and the sober black of his Service tie were enlivened by the blood-red of his Spanish-bought shirt and his red tan shoes, he was inevitably arrested by two Military Policemen on the very steps of the Club. But his amazing luck still held. The New Zealand High Commissioner was just stepping out of his car at the Club steps, and Chalky called to him. He came across, and without waiting for Chalky's explanation, persuaded the two MPs that Chalky was a personal friend and his especial protégé, and he would appreciate it if they would unhand him in fairly short order.

Seeing no one he knew in the Club, he took a taxi back to his digs, where he deemed it prudent to resume complete civilian garb.

Then there was the matter of returning to operations. Chalky was back on ops the next day after his return to Biggin Hill, his very first show taking him over the same area in which he had been shot down. He did "a few more shows" before being called up by Malan, who told him, crossly, that some Air Ministry type had declared that there was a clause in the Geneva Convention prohibiting ex-POWs from returning to operations. Chalky protested luridly that it was all a lot of nonsense, that he wasn't really an ex-POW, but had merely spent a little time in enemy-controlled territory, and that if that ruled him out of Ops, the whole RAF would have to be stood down. But Air Ministry was Air Ministry, and while Malan got that one sorted out, Chalky was sent around several RAF Commands to tell them how to become successful escapers/evaders — "given my luck," he always added modestly.

Malan evidently argued to some purpose on Chalky's behalf, for he returned to and remained on operations almost until the end of hostilities, winning a Mention in Despatches, a DFC and promotion to Flight Lieutenant. His squadron was posted to 135 Wing, which was based for a time at Merville with Group Captain D.J. Scott's 123 Wing, 2nd Tactical Air Force.

With Group Captain Scott, Flight Lieutenant L.P. Griffiths and a Czechoslovakian colonel, he entered Dunkirk on a purely speculative exploration into the possibility of its being surrendered, and was thus one of the first four Allied officers to enter that battered port town since the British evacuation in June, 1940.

Chalky White arrived home in November, 1945. Group Captain Scott had expressed concern over what effect their experiences would have on these survivors of flak storms and fighters. He knew so well the dual existence which took men from the rural peace of fighter and bomber fields all over England and, in a mere hour or so, plunged them into infernos of battle, mayhem and sudden death, and then, if they were sufficiently quick, skilful and lucky, dropped them back into that other reality, in that quiet English countryside, and did it again, and again, and again, times without number, years without end, so that they became accustomed to living two widely disparate, utterly incompatable lives at once. He wondered how they would ever again be able to settle into the old, pre-war lifestyle.

In Chalky's case, he need have felt no such concern.

Chalky went back to shearing within a month of coming home. Out of training for such work, he found that, (to quote his own words), "I sweated too much, and I thought there must be an easier way to make money; so I went and bought five trainloads of sheep without any money...."

He sold them again at a price which enabled him to pay for them before the vendors had time to become alarmed, and which showed a good profit. With the profit, he set himself up on his own farm.

He is, today, a rather more than ordinarily successful sheep farmer, shearing some 12,000 sheep and running about 1200 head of cattle. The personal qualities which served him so well in war were no less useful in peace. He was prepared to take risks — but he backed them up and ensured their success with muscle and sweat and vigour, and that indomitable and somewhat impatient spirit of "give-it-a-go".

At sixty-seven years of age, he is still a formidable character, still exudes self-confidence, still looks at the world with fearless eyes, still regards life as a series of challenges. It doesn't bother him. That's how life is. He doesn't boast about his accomplishments, or feel that he needs to. It's probably that impatience which is the key to all that he ever did, or ever was. When Chalky White has a job on, any kind of job, you can feel it. Anything that isn't part of the job is an interruption. You might say that when you see him physically or spiritually on the run, sooner or later you realise — Chalky White isn't running away from anything. He's running to get back to something, so that he can complete whatever it was that he started out to do. He's been doing it all his life.

They didn't have a hope of detaining a man like that.